A Place Too Small for Secrets

The Arts Council
An Chomhairle Ealaíon

The publishers gratefully acknowledge the financial assistance
of the Arts Council/An Chomhairle Ealaíon

First published in 2002 by Marino Books
16 Hume Street Dublin 2
Tel: (01) 661 5299; Fax: (01) 661 8583
E-mail: books@marino.ie
An imprint of Mercier Press
Website: www.mercier.ie

Trade enquiries to CMD Distribution
55A Spruce Avenue
Stillorgan Industrial Park
Blackrock County Dublin
Tel: (01) 294 2560; Fax: (01) 294 2565
E.mail: cmd@columba.ie

ISBN 1 86023 146 2
10 9 8 7 6 5 4 3 2 1

A CIP record for this title is available
from the British Library

Cover design by Marino Books

Printed in Ireland by ColourBooks,
Baldoyle Industrial Estate, Dublin 13

A Place Too Small for Secrets

Paddy Kennelly

For Kate, for Alan and Mary,
for John and Maebh, and for Ryan and Colm

JIM THE RUBBISH MAN

A place too small for secrets, some might say.
Who, here, would know and not reveal the knowing?
Only the wind?
Only the hungry fox
Sniffing my rubbish dump for bits and scraps
Of living souls?
Only the priest in his box?

A place too small for secrets, you might say.
But you'd be wrong.

I know
Who stole the tuna from Miss Eily's shelves.
Not Hannah Grogan,
Though Miss Eily swears that it was she;
And not the Widow Connor,
Though hunger stalks her every step
And saps the spunk from her six sons.

You could be guessing till the cows come home
And never once suspect
The lady with the quick and thieving hands.

Her name?
You'll not hear it from me.
But this much I will say:
She made the very same mistake
With each and every empty tuna tin
As the sly boy, the Holy Joe,

Who brought the first French letter to Knockore
And thought, afterwards, the evidence was safe,
Wrapped up in tissue paper
At the bottom of his bin.

Séamus Mac An tSionnaigh

I let the facts speak.

My wife, Eibhlís, had ten children
In twelve years.

During her pregnancy with Séamus Óg –
Her fifth child, our first son –
She was confined to bed for ten weeks.

While pregnant with Ruairí and Orla –
Her second set of twins –
She was in mortal danger from clotting of the blood.

At the birth of her last child, Eimear,
She suffered a mild stroke.
A stern gynaecologist warned
Another pregnancy would be fatal.

I love my wife.

And so it was that I,
Séamus Mac An tSionnaigh,
Schoolteacher,
Renowned local historian
(I let the facts speak),
President of the Knockore Branch
Of the League of Decency,
Went with my wife on a brief holiday
To her former home in England

And returned with a gross of condoms
Hidden on my person.
(That was the time
When such items were still contraband,
Before the pagans of the Liberal Agenda
Brought this country to its knees.)

My conscience is clear on this matter,
I believe I am in the state of grace.
After all, the facts proclaim
Mine was a special case.

Eibhlís Bean Uí Shionnaigh

We first met
In Bradford, my native town.
He was working as a bus conductor
During his long summer holidays from school.
I was a student of Roman archaeology
At the University of Leeds.
I saw him on the bus and fell in love
Before I asked him for my ticket.
He was James Fox then,
And I, Elizabeth Bliss.

In three weeks we were married
And he brought me here to this remote place
In the south-west of Ireland
Far from my own people,
Far from my student life,
From Herculaneum and Pompeii.
Was that the hardest thing he asked me to do?

The people here are good people,
Friendly, hospitable and humorous.
I would not now exchange these friends
For − as they would put it − love nor money.
Hannah Grogan, for example,
Comes every afternoon to my home
And, for three hours, while I take a nap,
Babysits my large brood.
The only payment she will take
Is the liberty of warning me

That my husband is like all men –
A brute when it comes to women.

My large brood?
Ten children in twelve years?
It seemed once I had been vomiting
Ever since I set foot in Ireland.
My health failed, though thankfully –
Now that the pregnancies are over –
I believe I am recovering my strength.
Constant pregnancies and failing health –
Was that the hardest thing he asked me to do?

I love my husband.
He is a good man –
A good father to my brood.

I love my children.
I would not – as my neighbours might put it –
Send wan of 'em back.

My name, now, is Eibhlís Bean Uí Shionnaigh.
It is a name I can't pronounce.
Eibhlís?
Eye-leash?
Oil-l-l-leesh?
It is their thick 'L's that defeat me,
As when they say, 'It is a l-lovel-ly day.'

Bean Uí Shionnaigh?
Banee Hiunic?

Ba-knee Who-nig?
B'ny Hunig?

Eibhlís Bean Uí Shionnaigh,
I can spell your name
But I can't pronounce you.
Are you me?
Am I you?

How can I say who I am
When I can't even say my name?

Sometimes in bed at night
I try to befriend you,
Oil-l-l-leesh Ba-knee Who-nig,
But you remain a stranger to me.

Oh what has become of Elizabeth Bliss?

To live with a name I can't pronounce –
That's the hardest thing he asked me to do.

And the second-hardest?
After some time
I became attuned to their accent
And they to mine,
But even now I still cannot decipher
Some of their wild metaphors,
Their outlandish turns of phrase.
I live among a people
Whose words I cannot always understand.

For instance . . .
Once, on hearing I was pregnant yet again,
Hannah Grogan exclaimed,
'Tell Maca Tunic he's the devil painted,
Tell him he's tearin' th'arse of it.'
This was her way, I later learned,
Of rebuking my dear husband
For, as she believed, excessive sexual demands.

And when she said,
'Tell him – from now on
He must milk outside the bucket',
How was I to know
This was her metaphor to recommend
A means of contraception much in vogue
With Romans in Pompeii long ago –
Coitus interruptus?

EIBHLÍS BEAN UÍ SHIONNAIGH

It was a good lecture my beloved gave
To the Knockore Heritage Society
On 'The Course of Resistance to English Rule
In the Barony of O'Connor'.

No doubt there was some blowing
Of the Irish trumpet, some slight exaggeration
Of the valour of O'Connor's clan,
But this was understandable,
Given the audience on the night,
Though when I heard Séamus on about
The special contribution of *his* ancestors,
I was reminded of Hannah's words:
'Men are a terror for boastin',
To listen to 'em, you'd swear
They could sweep all before 'em.
What harm, but there's only
The wan quick burst in 'em, and after that
They're flat as pancakes.'

And it occurred to me
That, in the matter of resisting the invader,
Irishmen had proved true to form,
With each quick sally forth
Followed by a meek capitulation:
The ruined walls are there to prove it.

Somewhat more surprising, in his lecture,
Was the underlying anti-English sentiment,
Especially as his Bradford wife was listening in.
'I must have him modify his tone somewhat,'
I thought, 'I must have him strive
Towards objectivity. After all,
We, the English, can't be blamed
If the Irish character proved so amenable
To a policy of bribes and threats.'
Again I thought of Hannah's wisdom:
'A little bit of refusal here –
The headache, in bed –
And a tasty little morsel there –
Custard, after dinner –
Will soon bring the most stubborn of men
Round to your way of thinkin'.'

Hannah was right, as usual,
And, having followed her advice,
I don't envisage Séamus ever lecturing
On the course of his resistance
To my rule.

Nora Grogan

I had fractions for homework,
So I asked my mum to explain
The lowest common denominator.
She said, ''Tis what you aim for
When you're dealin' with men.'

The Recent Proposal of Séamus Mac An tSionnaigh, Resigned Chairperson and Ex-member of the Knockore Branch of the League of Decency, to the Knockore Heritage Society

My friends,
Of late I have been contemplating
The etymology of 'Knockore'.
It has been a troubled contemplation.

'Knockore':
From the Gaelic, 'An Cnoc Óir',
Meaning 'The Hill of Gold',
So called because, in bygone days,
The sinking sun would lend a golden hue
To wheatfields nestling on the hillside –
Nature's compliment
To the husbandry of our farming ancestors.

Some scholars dispute this:
They insist the Gaelic name is 'An Cnoc Fhómhair' –
'The Harvest Hill'.
But whichever etymology is accepted,
The thrust is still the same:
To draw attention to the fruitful work
Of men long gone – our forefathers,
Who turned a barren hillside
Into a land of golden grain.

We are proud of this name –
Our designation as a race

Which so successfully confronted
The challenges of furze and bog
That even Nature itself
Stooped to pay compliment.

This name applauds us
For being who we are,
Points us to a way
Trodden by others for a thousand years.

And yet . . .
Is there a danger here
That we, who so congratulate ourselves
On an illustrious ancestry,
Who so publicly proclaim our loyalty
To an ancient ethic,
Might seek to demand of others,
Not similarly minded as ourselves,
Adherence to the standards of our past?

The flattering image is lethal
When it becomes a living thing, suspicious and resentful
Of every new departure from itself.
It will not tolerate scrutiny.
Its face is public, and it does not mind
If the values it publicly insists upon are not upheld in private.

Knockore, your name invites me
To a smug appraisal of myself,
But as I advance in years,
The less inclined I am to self-applause.

The outward signs of smugness
Made visible in me
Are cant, intolerance and hypocrisy.

My friends:
There is another etymology
Which I invite you to consider.

According to mythology
(Which I am increasingly disposed
To favour more than facts
When broaching the spirit of a place),
Our hill, in Gaelic, should be called
'An Cnoc Áir' – 'The Hill of Slaughter'.
This is because, in prehistoric times
And on this very spot,
The Fianna, led by Fionn Mac Cumhaill,
Engaged in battle an army of invaders.
And on the day, Fionn, so the legend goes,
Was overcome with bloodlust
And did not cease his killing
Even when the enemy surrendered,
Believing that thereby they would be spared.
Fionn slaughtered till blood reddened the fields,
Till the yellow furze blushed red,
Till even the river flowing down the hill ran red,
So that forever after it was called
'An Abhann Dearg' – 'The Red River'.

A slaughterer of men was Fionn that day;
He turned a deaf ear to every pitiable cry for mercy.

A slaughterer of men
And a leader of men, too, whose motto was:
'*Gloine ár gcroí*
Agus neart ár ngéag
Agus beart do réir ár mbriathar' –
'Purity of heart
And strength of limb
And fidelity to our bond'.

I ask you,
Where was Fionn's purity that day,
When every plea for mercy
Served further to arouse his lust for blood?
And of what value strength of limb
If used in slaughter's service?
And where his bond
To a surrendered foe?

The myth recounts
That when at last the killing was all done,
Fionn surveyed the mayhem and the slaughter
And, cupping his face in his bloodstained hands,
Wept inconsolably.

What, then, shall we say of Fionn?
Shall we say
He was the bravest warrior in all our Gaelic lore?
Or shall we say he was a hypocrite
Who marched to war with prayer on his lips
And slaughter in his heart?

Or shall we say he was a man?

Who wept
At the red evidence of evil in his heart;
A man too honest
To scurry to the past
For the comforting, forgiving lie,
Yet brave enough
Always to retain a vision of himself
As pure and strong and true.

My friends,
The name 'An Cnoc Óir'
Consigns us to a history
At once flattering and false.
The name 'An Cnoc Áir'
Insists that we confront our darker side –
The lust for slaughter in our hearts –
But it also offers us the privilege
Of aspiring to a higher destiny.

I therefore propose we change our name
From 'Knockore' to 'Knockawer'.
Thank you for your attention.

Postscript: This proposal was rejected without debate, on a show of hands. It was supported only by Mac An tSionnaigh and by Jim the Rubbish Man.

Hannah Grogan

We boarded Fitzpatrick's bus at half past eight in the morning
And headed off from the Corner
On the annual pilgrimage to Knock,
Complete with our rosary beads,
Our flasks of tea,
Our sandwiches and buns.

Moses Coffey – chairman of the Holy Joes
Since Mac An tSionnaigh handed in his badge –
Was in command.
He took the job seriously, but for all that
I wouldn't trust him as far as I'd throw him –
He's a man the same as the rest of 'em.
'We'll say a Rosary to set us on our way,' he said.

That was only the start of the Rosaries –
There were plenty more to come.

We stopped at a picnic area somewhere outside Galway
For a bite to eat and a pee.
When I saw Moses headin' for the gents –
May God forgive me, but I couldn't help myself,
He's so full of piety – I said,
'Remember, Moses, you can shake him only once.
After that you're playing with yourself.'
He blushed.
'That's no way for a lady to talk,' he said.

Confessions and Mass in Knock,
The Stations of the Cross, another Rosary,
Our empty Nash's lemonade bottles
Filled with Knock holy water,
Tea and sandwiches and buns,
And one last pee before
Turning for the Corner in Knockore.

Somewhere outside Galway on the journey home,
Just as we had finished another Rosary,
The temper started risin' in me,
And I said I'd have it out with her.

So up I goes to her seat
And stands before her, bold as brass.
'Miss Eily,' I says, 'is it true you're tellin' all your customers
That I'm the one behind your disappearin' tunas?'
She blushed.

There was silence in the bus
While she squirmed in her seat.

'And did you tell your customers,' says I,
'That your seven times great-grandfather
Was hauled before the courts for stealin' sheep?
And that Maca Tunic has the proof of it
In documents sent down from Dublin?
And that your thieving ancestor
Was, for his crime, transported to Van Diemen's Land,
Where he begot a race of beggars
Who'd pick the eye out of your own head

24

While you weren't lookin'?
And if you want the proof of *that*,
All you have to do is go there –
'Tis only a short hop from the butt of Australia –
And you'll find plenty biddies wanderin' around,
The spittin' image of yourself,
All with long noses and no man.'

She started sniffling then, if you don't mind.
'And as for your disappearin' tunas,' I said,
When I was already halfway back to my seat:
'You can stick 'em up your arse!'

What was in the bus
Gave a great 'Ye-hay!' at that.

Moses Coffey got all hot and bothered
At Miss Eily's tears: 'Now, now,' he said,
'There's no call for such language, Hannah Grogan,
And I'd ask you to remember
That we're on our annual pilgrimage to Knock.'
Then, turnin' to her ladyship, he said,
'Don't be too upset, Miss Eily,
At this minor altercation.
There's bound to be the odd troublemaker
On long pilgrimages like this.
I'll do my best, as leader of the group,
To calm her down. But don't expect too much –
Didn't Moses himself have trouble
With the bickering Jews on their pilgrimage
From slavery to the Promised Land?'

'And if I was you, Moses Coffey,' I said,
'I wouldn't crow too much
About my namesake from the Bible.
He might have got the slabs of law
Upon the Holy Mount, but when he saw
The Jews up to their antics,
Wasn't he the very man
To fly into such a towerin' rage
That in wan go he broke all ten?'

After that things quietened down.
I'd had my say; that was enough for me.

We were back in our Promised Land at a quarter to eleven
After a most enjoyable day – except that, ever since,
I'm half-sainted from the power of prayer.

Miss Eily Shea

I own the Spar shop on Main Street;
I own the Yard and the Mill;
I own the lane called Miss Eily's;
I own a house on the Hill.

Though mostly I'm very happy
As monarch of all I survey,
I have these moments of madness
When I'd pitch it all away.

POLISHED PAT

Meetings can be arranged
For the wrong place, at the wrong time.

As, for example, at Gortagleanna Bridge
On May the twelfth, 1921,
Where Walsh and Lyons and Dalton,
Three members of the North Kerry Flying Column,
Met for some forgotten reason.
And as they chatted there,
Who, by some curse of fate, should chance the way
But a lorryload of Tans.
They dragged our boys inside a ditch
And shot them there like dogs.

A Celtic cross marks where they died,
And their names are still revered
In ballad and in song.

Or, for example, in Miss Eily's Lane
At three in the morning, just an hour ago,
Where I met with Majella Mai O'Leary
For an adulterous tryst.
And while we sported there,
Who, by some curse of fate, should chance the way
But Foncy Allman, the insomniac.
Just one brief glance,
And he knew everything he needs to know
To hug the centre stage in Knockore pubs
For months to come.

Just one brief glance
To furnish names and place and hour –
The details he'll fill in himself.
They'll grow more graphic with each telling –
Or mocking, depending on his whim
Or on what any audience might require
For entertainment on a winter's night.

Tell me, my friend –
A meeting with the Tans in Gortagleanna
Or with Allman in Miss Eily's Lane –
Which is your preferred end?

This much is sure:
No Celtic cross will mark my place of shame,
No ballads will be written to my name.

THE BALLAD OF POLISHED PAT
(AUTHOR UNKNOWN)

This ballad was doing the rounds in Knockore and was sent anonymously, through the post, to Mrs Eleanor Foley, Polished Pat's wife.

Patrick H. Pearse was our hero
In the battle of Nineteen Sixteen
When he lowered the colours of England
And hoisted the banner of green.
St Patrick is fondly remembered
For bringing the Faith to our shore
But a Patrick more famous than any
Is our own Polished Pat from Knockore.

Chorus

 There was never a Patrick so dandy
 As the Patrick who lived in our town;
 In his shoes you could see your reflection,
 While Brylcreem adorned his crown.
 There was always a crease in his trousers,
 He had a new shirt every day,
 But he lost all the spit and the polish
 In the arms of Majella Mai.

Some heroes are famed for their vision –
Like Tone who tried hard to unite;
And some are remembered for valour –
I think of O'Neill in the fight;

Some heroes are noted for cuteness –
O'Connell with his coach and four;
But one is renowned for his polish –
Our own Polished Pat from Knockore.

Chorus

Some of our men disappointed:
O'Connell, he threatened in vain,
The meeting in Clontarf he cancelled,
And sent us all back home again;
Parnell had his frolics with Kitty,
And left us divided and sore,
And poor Polished Pat came a cropper
In a back lane in lovely Knockore

Chorus

O come all ye tender young maidens,
A word of advice take from me:
Don't be fooled by the Brylcreem and polish
When a man puts his hand on your knee.
Beware of the tie and the collar,
Beware of the spick and the span,
And if you want proof of this lesson,
Our own Polished Pat is your man.

Chorus

Majella Mai O'Leary

Why are men so afraid
Of knowing themselves
That, on the instant of discovery,
Lust turns limp?

Why will not men rejoice
For the moment of ecstasy,
Preferring instead to weep
Over reputations of sand?

Why do some men boast
Of conquests never made,
While others seek to deny
Their finest hour?

Why do men ridicule
Anonymously, in song,
The sweet, illicit tryst
Wishing its way through their dreams?

FONCY ALLMAN

'I could name names', I used to say –
Hinting for the thousandth time
At tasty morsels of scandal.
'I could name men and women who,
Come the darkness of the early hours,
Get up to all sorts of weird shenanigans,
Though, in the light of day, you'd swear
Butter wouldn't melt in their mouths.
But what these people do
In the early-morning alleys of Knockore,
Where I patrol while all the world sleeps,
Is no one's business but their own.'
So – I'll name no names.

Even that might suffice
For a slack night in winter,
When an audience, for entertainment, could explore
Outrageous possibilities of sin
And I, at last, would have a part to play.

And then, my lucky break – that night
I caught my polished friend.
From that very moment his name was mine
And I made the most of it.
No hinting now, in this, my hour of fame.
I named the place and I supplied the name.

There was a type of homage paid to me.
It was expressed in belly laughs and loud guffaws,
And if it turned out transient in the end
And proved its insincerity when men grew bored,
What matter? For that one, glorious season,
Even when I'd return to my empty house,
My head was loud and addled with requests
To tell my story one more time.

And isn't anything better than the deep
Silence waiting for me once again at the front door,
Insisting I must soon confront myself?

I wonder why I cannot sleep.

Foncy Allman

Only to myself would I admit the truth:
During those midnight strolls,
Which took me the full round,
Starting in Main Street, at my own home,
Then southwards through the Glen,
Then up Pill Hill, and down the Old School Road,
Then northwards through Cows Lane,
Before making it back home again
Some one hour twenty minutes after starting out –
During the thousand times
I did that clockwise trip,
I never once – not once
Until the night with Polished Pat –
Was witness to a single incident
That might be worth a minute's gossip.

Only a tom-cat on the prowl,
Or the passing headlights of a car,
Or the bright streak of a falling star,
Or the hooting of a barn owl
Had I for company.

And nothing else to hear or see.

Unless – unless one counts the night
I, on a whim, walked anti-clockwise,
Going, first, from Main Street to Cows Lane.
There, passing by the Widow Connor's house
At ten past two, I chanced to see

A slit where the curtains of her bedroom window
Had not been fully drawn.
Her light was on.
Some pagan impulse prompted me
To steal up quietly and peep in.
I saw her in her nightdress, on her knees,
Rigid in prayer, erect, her arms not resting
On the bedside, and her eyes focused
Upwards with unblinking stare.

I left her there.

And journeyed on until
I was back home again
And was about to turn my key,
But then decided otherwise.
Back to Cows Lane I went,
At half past three in the morning.
The opening in the curtains was still there,
The light still on –
And still she was at prayer
And still, too, that unblinking stare.

Not a single word of this have I made known,
Nor ever will, for what goes on
Between the Widow Connor and her God
Is no one's business but her own.

Majella Mai O'Leary

Sometime along the way I changed,
Though when, I can't precisely say.
All I know is it was gradual
And unspectacular as growing grass,
Which one day, when the time is right,
Invites you to get out and mow the lawn.

But two events stand out:
That sudden downpour needled with hail
Which sent me scurrying to the nearest shelter
In, it so happened, our parish church.
Leaning against a pillar there, drawing my breath,
I thought I had the place all to myself,
Till I was suddenly aware of someone
Far up, near the altar. It was a woman – crying,
Yes – definitely crying. She turned and looked
On hearing my sharp intake of breath,
And for a moment frozen in time
Eleanor Foley's eyes blazed into mine.

And the very next day – that visit
From Father Charles McGettigan, our new PP,
Who I was ready to believe was latest in a line
Of interfering clergymen come to chide.
But when I opened the door he just stood there
And said, 'Majella Mai O'Leary – I want you to know
Jesus Christ thought you were a woman worth dying for.'
Then he turned on his heel and left.

And yet, the change being gradual,
It was long before the people of Knockore
Grew in amused and cynical bewilderment
At this notorious but repentant sinner
Each morning resting her left hand in her right
To receive from Charles McGettigan PP
The body of the Man who died for her;
And longer still before some local wit
Gave me the nickname that has stuck like glue:
Charlie's Angel.

ELEANOR FOLEY

I saw her coming up the path
Looking suitably demure
And I couldn't contain the scream:
'Get out, you whore!'

She stood there, said she was sorry.
How changed, her eyes!
But my heart would not believe
Her meek apologies.

And while she asked forgiveness,
I felt my fingers itch
To redden her brazen cheek –
The bitch! The bitch!

And when I let her have it,
Did she turn the other one?
I can't say, because I turned –
Straight back in home.

Lord, you are cruel on women
Who struggle by the Book.
I've always been the righteous one
And she the slut – but look

How her quiet composure
Is now for all to see
While I feed on the frenzy
Feeding on me.

JACK THE RAM

What, oh what
Has come over Majella Mai?
She used to be, 'You may';
Now she's, 'You may not.'

STEPHEN HOLLY

Every afternoon at two, weather permitting –
And all I need is the barest whiff of a sun
Watering its way through the clouds –
I come to my front door and, first, survey the scene.
Five or six of the curious might turn out,
Scattered along the main street of Knockore,
To witness the event. I salute them
And they acknowledge, reverentially.

The secret, then, is in the wind-up.
First, you turn your back to the sun,
Arms resting on the wall, legs outstretched,
As if being frisked. Now, twist your head
Gingerly, under your right shoulder,
For a fleeting glimpse of the sky.
But – and here's the tricky bit – only for long enough
To start a tickle in your nostril.
Make sure to avert your gaze before the urge
Becomes too strong – a bit like sex, where
Timing, too, is all-important,
Except that this is harder to control
And requires more getting used to.

Repeat the dose a dozen times or so:
You'll find with each successive glimpse
The tickle will intensify
Until, eventually, it extracts,
In the effort to suppress it,
A series of aborted grunts and snorts,

Sometimes even a pawing of the ground,
Like an angry Spanish bull.
This is the prelude to the main event.

At last you'll feel the body stiffening,
The muscles going into spasm,
The tickle in the nostrils driving you
To somewhere between pain and ecstasy.

Then – but not till then – you can let fly.

I say now, without fear of contradiction,
That those who come to listen and to see
Are never disappointed when at last
The main street rattles to my glorious expulsion
Of tickling demons. And then, the demonstration over,
And the village settled back into itself,
I wave goodbye to my admirers
And return indoors,
Leaving them to marvel and discuss.

And in years to come, when people will remember
The characters in Knockore long ago,
They'll talk of Polished Pat and Charlie's Angel,
Of men who couldn't sleep at night and so
Must walk the streets at every hour;
And my name will be mentioned too
In every acre of this land.

My sneeze will be my footprint in the sand.

PADDY DEE

And if you'd know how *I* will be remembered
Go to the Grotto out the Old School Road.
Face north. Walk fifty-seven paces on,
Until you reach the cluster of five trees
That we call Steepee's Grove.
Go to the middle tree;
Examine carefully the bark.
On it, exactly five feet from the ground
You'll find a horseshoe hammered in.
Trapped between shoe and bark a piece of tin
Bears this inscription: 'Remember Paddy Dee
Who made this mark. June 1953.'

Bosco Collins

I was there – a young boy – on the day
Paddy Dee made his mark on the tree;
I was there – a grown man – with a saw
Cutting firewood for Trevor Steepee.

SIMPLE SIMON

And still I love to play
'Cowboys and Indians' – but just the other day
They held a powwow and they threw me out.
Said I was too old at twenty-one.
Said I was too big and I could never stay
Quiet when the cowboys were surrounding the Indians.
Said I always gave the game away.

I begged 'em to let me stay.
But no, they wouldn't. So I had to climb
Up on my horse for the last time
And ride off into the sunset. It was just the same
As in this picture I saw once, called *Shane*,
Where he gave 'em all a bellyful of lead.
And Shane himself would have been dead,
Except the boy outside the door
Warned him of the man behind him with a gun,
And just in time Shane wheeled and drew
And shot the low-down varmint. But Shane was wounded too
In his left hand. Still – he mounted up and rode away
And the boy kept callin' out to Shane to stay:
'Shane! Shane! Please stay! Come back! Come back!'
But Shane kept ridin' on – his left hand hangin' slack.

So, when I couldn't join them any more
I rode into the sunset, through Knockore,
Saying 'Giddy-up! Giddy-up!' and slappin' my side
As if it was the horse, my left hand slack, and I tried
To imagine I was Shane, and – yes! – from far away

Their voices came: 'Shane! Shane! Come back and stay!'
But no! I just kept ridin' on, though I could hear
Their 'Shane! Come back!' still ringin' in my ear.

And now I'll never play with 'em again.
Instead my hideout is Miss Eily's Lane,
Where I keep law and order for Knockore.
And I'm not Simple Simon any more –
I'm Simple Shane.

CRANKY ANDY BOO

'Castles fallin' and dunghills risin','
I always say to myself
When I behold the airs and graces
Of the upstarts from Cows Lane,
Who think their piss is perfume just because
They have a few bob in their pockets.
'Twasn't too long ago at all
When they didn't have as much
As would give you the itch.
I remember my own mother, God rest her,
Keepin' the sour milk for Sheila Grogan
To make the bread
For her ten hungry young wans;
And her husband, Oul' Tomasheen,
With his arse out through his trousers.
Now her daughter, Hannah, walks the street
With her nose in the air, and you'd be lucky
To have her bid you the time of day.

And then you have the snobs up on the Hill
Lookin' down on the rest of us.
Above all you have Miss Eily Shea,
Who still has her Communion money
And who passes my door each mornin'
On her way to open her shop,
All poshness and politeness,
And refusin' to talk the Queen's English.
'And how do you do, Mr Lenihan,
This rather chilly morning?' was her salute

No more than ten minutes ago.
Far from 'chilly' she was reared.
I'd had enough of it. 'I'm fine, Miss Shea,
Thank you for enquirin',' I said,
'Except for the matter of two piles,
One at either side of my arse.'
That knocked the hop out of her!
And off she skidaddled
As fast as her two legs would carry her,
So flustered and fustered
That she could hardly get the key in the door.
'Chilly' indeed! 'Twill be a long time
Before she gives me 'chilly' again.

To Miss Eily and her cohorts on the Hill,
And to the risin' dunghills in Cows Lane,
And to every nosey one the likes of you
Who wonders how I got my name,
I say 'Boo'.

Mickeen Connor (Under 12)

Hard to imagine that the aeroplane
Trailing across the sky just now
Is full of people who have never heard
About our final (Under 12s) tomorrow
When we, the Sons of Knockore,
Play Gale Rangers for the Schoolboys' Cup
At 3.15 (sharp) in Jim McMahon's field.

How could they
Have missed the posters everywhere
From Miss Eily's down to Steepee's Grove
Announcing date, event and venue, and in truth
Inviting the whole world to 'Come
And See the Cream of Ireland's Youth'?

JAMES WARD

One finds distasteful
The relish of the people of Knockore
For nicknames. And most so when
There is an inference of ridicule,
As, for example, their designation
Of the place I live in as 'Pill Hill',
Because its only – wealthy – residents
Are Miss Eily Shea, a spinster
(And note the slur imputed here)
And David Harrington and I,
With our wives and only sons –
This because we choose to differ from the people
Down below and not to breed like rabbits.

One would have thought more apt
A posture of respect
By way of gratitude to one
Who fled to England as a callow youth
From the hunger of the 'fifties,
Returning, decades on, a millionaire,
To launch a thriving business here,
And gainfully employ the populace
Of Knockore and surrounding villages.

And now – this most unpleasant business
Arising from a Gaelic football match
That I attended. (The first in thirty years,
And then only because my son

50

Was corner-forward on the schoolboys' team
Playing Gale Rangers on the day
And pleaded with me to go.)

I will concede that, as the match began,
I was a bored outsider. And yet, soon,
My blood responded to the Knockore boys,
Roused, perhaps, by memories of childhood days
Spent playing in that field, or else because
My son had scored a brilliant goal
Which stirred an ancient pride.
And then – my son was hit. The referee –
Outrageously – adjudged that he had fouled.
My temper welled up at this travesty.
Impulsively I joined a raucous chant
Of boos with my immediate neighbours:
'Will you open your fuckin' eyes, ref!'
I didn't hear myself saying,
And we each and every one demanded
That the cowardly bastard from the Gale
Be given his marching orders.

A blackguard from the opposition
Tapped me on the shoulder from behind,
Called me a biased hoor, declared that,
Only he was working in my factory,
He'd knock my skull in. I replied
He could keep his job no matter what,
But if he wanted a fight, now was the time.

We started at it there and then.
A brawl ensued, with men from either side
Involved. Fists flew. Blood flowed.
I've no desire to boast, but let me say
That I acquitted myself well and sent home
A good few scoundrels from the Gale
With thickened ears.
And I myself would have emerged unscathed
But for a grave miscalculation:
Believing the enemy to be at last defeated,
I lowered my fists, only to have some villain,
Seeing his chance, come at me from the side
And land a vicious blow on my left eye,
Which knocked me flat. Fair do's, however,
To the staunch supporters of Knockore;
The thug was apprehended and – as they
Would say – the shit was hammered out of him.

My dearest wife, on seeing my sorry state
When I returned home, was quite bewildered.
'Oh, James!' she said. 'What *did* come over you?'
The truth is I don't know. She now insists
I never more attend at such a gathering
Where, as she says, the savage natives congregate.

And, of course, one hangs one's head in shame
After the event. After all, one's sole reward
For such a lapse as this is a black eye –
That and the longest nickname in Knockore:
'The One Who Dropped One's Guard'.

Emma Ward

Sometimes, indeed, the natives do employ
A very charming, rustic turn of phrase.
Just now I've parted company
With a gritty little lady called –
Can you imagine this! – the Widow Connor.
(Does not the title perfectly encapsulate
The viewpoint of the Irish male
That women, even in widowhood,
Are merely an extension
Of a man's identity?)
She'd brought her young son, Michael,
Somewhat quaintly called 'Mickeen';
The little imp was crying
And on his arm the deep imprint of teeth
Showed why. This passing blemish, she complained,
Had resulted from a boyish altercation
With my darling, Francis Andrew,
Who will insist, despite repeated pleas,
Always on this – very Irish – means
Of self-defence. I told her that my boy
Would be most sternly spoken to in due course
When Mr Ward returned at the weekend
From a business trip abroad.
The little lady roused herself to say,
'But ma'am, 'twill be too late
If you put it off till when
Himself shows up –
Your youngster could have ate
What's in Knockore by then.'

DAVID HARRINGTON

I almost have it made.

Business is up by ten per cent,
And here in my house on the Hill
My new conservatory,
My snooker room and tennis court
Have gone down well.

Next on my list are
An indoor swimming pool
And a large solarium
Where, even in the Irish rain,
I can swim and acquire a tan –
Expensive luxuries, I fear,
Which will be a heavy drain
On my resources for some time.
But by this time next year,
I could be a happy man.

THE WIDOW CONNOR

Say what you will about
The One Who Dropped One's Guard,
But let me say this: he came today with jobs
For my two eldest in his timberyard.
The pay is generous and – to start them off,
He said – he gave them money in advance.
This evening they'll come home
To a heated kitchen and a table laid
With plenty food. After all these years,
We have it made.

GRACE HARRINGTON

Sometimes, lying awake at night,
Waiting for him to come to bed
When he has finished counting his pile,
When his accounts have all been read

And reread for reassurance
That by the end of the financial year
His riches will have grown still more,
I picture my sister, Eleanor,

Lying awake and thinking
Of Pat and Majella Mai,
Remembering over and over,
And I know she envies me

And that later she will visit
Her older sister and say
That her heart is broken
And that I should bless the day

I met the faithful David Harrington,
But my pride won't let me cry
Out the pain of my humiliation,
Won't let me say it is I

Who should envy her, for she, at least,
Has been rejected for flesh and blood
While I must make way for money,
And oh! where is the good

In swimming pools and snooker rooms
When the heart has turned to stone
And never will woman's body
Excite this David Harrington

The way that money does, and will
Somebody explain my urgent wish
That soon Miss Eily Shea will spot
My thieving hands possess her tins of fish.

Mossy Scully

What could be nicer on a summer's day
Than sitting at the back of the house
For hours on end, letting the sun
Infiltrate my seventy-year-old bones
While all the time the black songbird,
Perched on the ash tree halfway down the field,
Whistles his tune especially for me?
At my age
A man is entitled to indulge himself a little
By taking time off
To thank the Lord for his goodness
Instead of running about like a busy fool
Trying to put his two arms
Around the whole world.

And today I had a call from David Harrington –
His fifth in seven weeks –
Upping, one last time, his offer for the field
Where he would build his latest scheme –
An old folks' home 'to cater for the dying rich'.
I was sorry to refuse the thirty thousand pounds
With which he tempted me; it's an absurd
Sum for an acre you couldn't give away
A few years back. But still I ask myself:
What price the singing bird?

Cyril Coll (London)

Young I was that night, but hardly carefree,
For I didn't have the shilling
To take me to the dance,
So I stole a dozen eggs
From under Nell Cooney's hens
And sold them at the Corner Store
For twelve brown pence.

After the dance
I walked home Sarah Byrne,
And the sweetness of her kiss
Is with me still.

Now, each time I return,
Wealthy and respectable,
And aging, and fond of memories,
I seek out Nell Cooney
And tell her again the story
Of robbing her hatching hens.
And she calls me a little devil
When on her work-worn palm
I press twelve gold sovereigns.

JERRY FLEMING

Of course the business acumen
Of Cyril Coll escaped the rest of us,
Who were only left to wonder
How he raised the money for the dance.
But we, though poor, could always improvise.
So we gathered outside the hall
And there, under God's clear skies,
We danced our hearts out
To the notes that wafted from within;
Mossy Scully, I remember,
Loved any kind of music. He was a grand
Waltzer and every time a dance would end
He'd shout in the door: 'More band! More band!'

Bosco Collins

'No,' said Scully, when we had listened
To John B.'s *Sive* on the radio,
'It's not the sadness of the tale
That draws a tear to my eye,
Although I'll grant he tells it lovely.
Such tragic tales of love
Are commonplace, and anyhow
'Tis only make-believe.
But did you hear the music of the words –
A music no one uses now?
'Tis stretched there, dead and for real,
On the bare kitchen table,
And I'm wonderin' when
Will we ever hear the likes of it again?'

DAVID HARRINGTON

So at last, in complete exasperation,
I said, 'Old man, among the many things
You seem not to have learned
On your way to doddering senility
Is the value of a hard-earned pound.
And now I ask myself,
Where is your social conscience?
Or don't you know the day is fast approaching
When you, too, will be dumped
Into an old folks' home?
You don't expect your alcoholic son
To care for you? He'll sell this field
Before you stiffen in your bed
And piss the money at a pub-house wall.
But that, of course, won't have occurred to you
As you sit there and vegetate,
Learning nothing, nothing at all except
How to halt the march of progress.'
He winced at my assault and said,
'I must admit, it's absolutely true
That in all my years I've learned nothing
That could help a man like you.'

Which only went to prove my point of view.

DAVID HARRINGTON JUNIOR

When I grow up
I should like to be a judge.

For this you must, first, be confident
That you can always tell
The difference between
What's right, what's wrong.
My Mummy, I have judged,
Gives me the confidence
By constantly reminding me
That I am best at school,
Top of the class,
And called, as she says,
To be pre-eminent.

Then you must be fair but strict
In giving sentence.
My Daddy, I have judged,
Has taught me this;
Not, for example, to allow
Our very natural sympathy for the poor
Soften the blow of law
When they transgress.
What's theirs is theirs, so Daddy says,
But then, what's mine is mine.
And those who may think otherwise
Must be made toe the line.

MISS EILY SHEA

1

Here, in a private ward
Of St Joseph's Hospice for the Dying,
The evening sunlight of July
Pours a gentle benediction on me,
Drugged until pain is pleasant
And peace lingers like a resonance
Of what might have been
If only, all those years ago,
You had stayed.

2

Figures at my bedside:
An accountant, a solicitor,
Talking of stocks and shares,
Of investments that blossomed.
How poor must I become
Before they stop telling me
I am rich beyond my wildest dreams?

3

One thing only
Is more important
Than that we never cavorted
As man and wife:
Soon, now, I go to meet
Someone
Who loves me more
Than I loved you.

4

You must make a will, they say.
Why?
If you don't it will all be frittered away.

How shall I dispose of it?
As you would wish, they say.
I wish I had children to leave it to.
Then will it instead, they say.

MISS EILY SHEA

As for the money:

First, all my debts must be discharged
And all the costs incurred
Through illness, church and burial.
Then give to Hannah Grogan
Ten thousand pounds,
That when she speaks of me
She may have the good word.
Ten thousand pounds I leave
To Sarah Harrington,
My neighbour on the Hill,
That she may eat well.

There's more, much more, you say:
Select a children's charity
And give it all away.
Or would you have us here all day?

As for the property:

The place known as Miss Eily's Lane
I give to Simon Goggins,
Alias Simple Shane.
Sell all the rest,
The House, the Yard, the Shop, the Mill.
The proceeds give to Stephen Quill.

Witness my will.

CRANKY ANDY BOO

Only I'm a Catholic
I'd have burst out laughin'
While McGettigan was readin'
The Prayers at the Graveside
Over Miss Eily, for it was then
Her three first cousins
Took to pillaluwin' and bawlin'
And snifflin' and snufflin',
Givin' us enough tears to flood the Shannon
In a mighty show of lamentation
For a woman they hardly knew
And never bothered wance to visit
Until they got the whiff of her money.

But bein' a Catholic won't stop me
Chucklin' in the privacy of my home
At the hilarious consideration
Of the real tears that must have flowed
When the solicitor from Tralee
Hit 'em with the sad news of the will.

Can you imagine the scowl on their faces!
And the jaws droppin' in despair!
And the cursin' under their breath!
And the tearin' of hair!
I tell you,
I'd give my right hand to have been there.

Miss Eily's Lane

Do not suppose that I
Have many secrets to tell,
Though every once in a while
A genuine original,

Like Simple Simon,
Passes this way
And with his clownish
Antics brightens a day

Which otherwise would be
Predictable as lust or greed
Or whatever one selects
To make the heart bleed,

Or obsessed with itself.
Humans, for the most part,
Go on their mundane way,
Have perfected the art

Of being busy and unhappy.
Give me the smiling one,
Like Simple Simon,
Who opts for fun.

Conversations Overheard in Knockore

Between Cranky Andy Boo and Stephen Quill, former school buddies, on their first meeting for forty-seven years.

Boo: Stephen Quill! Don't tell me 'tis yourself I have?

Quill: It is indeed.

Boo: I don't believe you. I wouldn't know you from Adam.

Quill: Nor I you.

Boo: How long is it?

Quill: The most of fifty years.

Boo: Let me look at you . . . You lost the weight.

Quill: Well . . . I had cancer – a few years back. They had to cut out half the stomach.

Boo: 'Tis wan way of losin' it.

Quill: You're looking well yourself.

Boo: Ah, I don't know. The left hip has me crippled.

Quill: I suppose 'tis only to be expected. The age is there.

Boo: Will you talk sense, man? Isn't the right hip just as old and isn't it perfect?

Quill: Still, the mileage is up.

Boo: Let me look at you again. And where are you now?

Quill: Sydney, Australia.

Boo: And have you any notion of coming home?

Quill: Naw! I'm settled out there now. A wife. Two kids. Three grandchildren.

Boo: Sydney, you say?

Quill: Aye.

Boo: And what's the weather like out there?

Quill: Oh, we've got a lovely climate. Warm and sunny.

Boo: It never stopped pissin' here since you left.

Quill: After Sydney, you don't mind the rain.

Boo: The bloody land is swimmin'. It never dried up wance. You could stir it if you had a spoon. Fierce changes since you left.

Quill: Aye. All the old crowd are gone.

Boo: And they're buildin' an old folks' home out the School Road. Young Harrington, you know. He was tryin' to buy a site from Scully but the fool wouldn't sell.

Quill: And there'll be a funeral parlour to go with it – or so I've been told.

Boo: In our time, when we got sick, our own crowd looked after us.

Quill: That's true.

Boo: And when we died, we died in our own bed.

Quill: We did indeed.

Boo: And we were waked at home.

Quill: We were so.

Boo: And we had no hearse either – only to be shouldered out to the graveyard.

Quill: Changed times.

Boo: In our time, we died daycent. And we were waked daycent. Nothin' for the crowd that's dyin' now only old folks' homes and funeral parlours.

Allman: Did 'ou meet Quill since he landed?

Scully: I did so. He tells me he's out in Australia.

Allman: You know what brought him?

Scully: The boodle.

Allman: And a nice boodle it is.

Scully: Eight hundred thousand.

Allman: I've been thinkin'. He must have had a lovely way o' cuddlin' her.

Scully: 'Twas a pity he didn't pass on the secret.

Allman: We'd all be millionaires. And to think of all of 'em I cuddled in my time and not wan of 'em left me as much as a pissy-bed.

Boo: Wasn't Quill fast out of the traps all the same? Never bothered us wance for fifty years and then – all of a sudden! – out he shoots from nowhere. Like a knacky corner-forward.

Scully: Who'd blame him?

Boo: And the cut of him! The man is wore away to nothin'. He'll never last long enough to enjoy it.

Scully: I wouldn't say that now, Dan. He's lost a bit o' weight, that's all.

Boo: He's like a pull-through for a rifle . . . He had the boyo, you know.

Scully: So I heard.

Boo: Half the gut cut out.

Scully: He claims to have it licked.

Boo: Licked, my arse. The man isn't there at all.

Scully: He's gone a bit thin, that's all.

Boo: Thin, is it you say? You think you're thin, Mossy Scully. And I think I'm thin. But Stephen Quill is thinner than the two of us put together.

I wonder what possessed her.
Surely not love.
Where was love's ruthlessness
In heaping scorn upon her old man's plea
To wait until he died
Before she made the bastard from Cows Lane
New lord and master of the Hill?
Where was love's deference to my shame
Of never knowing who my mother was?
Where was love's understanding
That if the Hill could not be mine
Then I must go,
An outcast from the jibes,
And from the lowliness of bastardy
In Knockore long ago.
And where was love's readiness,
When all else failed, to gather traps
And come away with me?

So what possessed her then?
A mind deceived with pain?
Or dotage in old age?
Or festering regret?
I like to think it was a burning rage
At that old man who, surely now,
Must squirm in his grave
To know that after all the years
The bastard has returned
To claim, if not the Hill,

73

Then all the proceeds of its sale –
And all according to his daughter's will.

As for myself?
Well, then – I ran before,
And turned my back forever on Knockore;
Now, before Daddy's cousins think of law
To dispute my rightful claim,
I'll grab the money
And I'll run again.

BRIGID ALLMAN

'Even the bed you sleep in isn't yours',
She was fond of reminding me
When she was home on holidays
From her nursing post in England.
I'd look at my husband, Foncy,
Who, fearful of his older sister,
Always kept his eyes down at these times.
'What will we do when she retires?' I'd ask,
In the privacy of the bed that wasn't ours.
His answer was always the same:
'We'll jump that fence when we come to it.'

We did come to that fence
But Allman was no man at all
And his eyes were always down
While his wife was reduced, diminished
To the status of a homeless waif
Who didn't even own the bed she slept in.
I begged him come away, but he was adamant:
This house was where his father died
And his father's father; he'd die there too,
And that was the end of it.

That was the end of it.

One morning, thirty years ago,
Scared out of my wits
At what I was about to do,
I got on the Limerick bus,

A woman on the run to nowhere,
And took flight from her
And from her spineless brother
And from my native place forever.
A trusted friend who keeps in touch
Tells me that since she died,
He walks the streets by night,
As though afraid to occupy the bed
That once he feared to claim his own.
Of me he never speaks,
Nor does he know my story
Since I took the Limerick bus that day –
And in truth there isn't much to tell.
How could there be, of someone
Whose greatest act of daring
Was to run away?

NORA HANSON

May God forgive me on this Christmas Eve,
Which sees me contemplatin'
Not the little fella in the crib
But, there on my kitchen table,
The pile of warm clothes
I bought with borrowed money
To cover my freezin' childer.

What came over me at all
After fifteen years or longer
Of strugglin' to make ends meet?
Was it the day that's in it
That drove me to this madness?
All I know is – I went out
Intendin' to spend the tenner
That I had scrimped and scraped for,
But instead of goin' shoppin'
I veered left
And into Harrington to borrow money.
Then off I went and bought all round me
Clothes straight off the rack
As if there was no tomorrow.
Oh little fella in the crib,
How am I goin' to pay it back?

NED McCORMACK

You are free to speculate
Why a man of fifty-seven,
Blessed with a salmon's health,
An athlete's body and an inquiring mind,
A veteran of the War of Independence,
When he made it his business to shoot the Tan,
Who gave the order for Knockore to be burned,
And who, later, sided with the 'Staters
When we Irish turned on each other –
You are free to speculate why this man
Should, when the fighting was all over,
Rear a family of seven sons and then,
One day in 1954,
Take to his bed and stay there
And not get up again
Except, maybe, for a few days in July each year
When the sun was splitting the stones
And the bedroom which would be his world
For thirty years became insufferably warm.

You are free to speculate, and for that
You might consider thanking me
And those who fought
That one day you'd be free.

Only, when you speculate,
Don't reach the wrong conclusion.
Don't, for example, say
The man must be depressed

To take to the bed like that.
Come into my kitchen any day
('Tis just below my bedroom)
And, if you're lucky,
You might hear me hum my favourite tune:
'If I Were a Blackbird'.
Or climb the stairs and visit:
You'll find me doing the puzzles,
Or listening to the radio,
Or chatting to my eldest son,
Who brings me all the news
And keeps me more in touch
Than many up and about.
Or you might find me
Staring out the bedroom window
Watching the people come and go –
The children of those I killed for
And would have died for.

Watching them come and go –
The children of a new and cowardly age.
See how they doff their hats
To the man with the round collar,
As stylishly as any craven Paddy
Kowtowed before the landlord, Henryson,
Who pushed his luck too far,
Evicted one tenant too many,
And is now, for his trouble, sproutin' daisies
In an unmarked grave.

The new man, Charles McGettigan,
Would step off the pedestal, I hear,
Only he won't be let. One day,
When they tire of this new master,
They may turn on him,
Blaming him for being
What they insist he be.
But for now McGettigan will do,
Instead of Kenneth Henryson,
To cater for that part of us
Which, like any fearful tenant,
Would kowtow to a feared authority.
Where, then, was the good
In changing those who ruled us
When we didn't change ourselves?
Now I know
I fought the wrong fight
And the gun I turned on the Tan
Who ordered Knockore to be burned
I should have aimed
At something deep within myself.
I fought the wrong fight
And so, where landlords ruled,
The clergy now hold sway,
Feeding the need in Irish hearts
To be subservient. And how does one
Fight that? If you tell me
Then I'll get up today.

CRANKY ANDY BOO

And I say, 'Boo', too,
To Charles McGettigan, PP,
Who, even as I speak,
Is chatting openly in the street
With that harlot, Charlie's Angel.
What kind of example is that
From a man with the round collar?
Only yesterday I saw him swappin' jokes
With Jassy Groarke, the by-child,
Whose mother, Mary, bold as brass,
Parades him through the main street of Knockore
Without as much as a blush.
And I remember my own father
Tellin' how Nora Mary Quill
Was driven from the village in disgrace
On the very day she brought her baby,
Stephen, into this world.
Those were the times
When you could leave the key in the door
The round of the clock
Safe in the knowledge that
Not even a spoon of sugar would be stolen.
Knockore Church was full each Sunday
For the half-nine and the half-eleven,
And for the Holy Hour and Benediction
Wance a month. You'd be in mortal dread
Shufflin' into the confession box
If you'd anythin' daycent to confess.
What the priest said, went,

And people lived in fear
Of being caught in the act of misbehavin'.
'Tis no wonder, now, the Church is banjaxed
When the clergy are ready to talk
To fatherless children and to loose
Women. McGettigan, of course,
Is afraid to crack the whip;
That man wouldn't say boo to a goose.

Myself and McCormack soldiered
Through the War of Independence
Till we grew close as brothers.
He was – a phrase he'd often use
Of others – an honourable man
Who insisted that the rules of war
Always be observed. We took different sides
When the Civil War began.
He would have shot me then
For, though honourable, he was ruthless
And, if the Cause demanded it,
He'd not let friendship stand in the way.
But at our first meeting when
That war was over, we hugged
Like brothers and renewed the bond
That had survived all – and still survived
Another thirty years, until the time,
A month or so before he took to bed,
We quarrelled at a game of cards.
He led the Five.
I reneged the Ace of Hearts
But – as I am an honourable man –
I did so only in devilment.
McCormack spotted the infringement
And flew into a rage. 'You cheat!'
He thundered. 'D'you take me for a fool!
Did you think I wouldn't spot it
When you broke the rule!'
Others at the table pointed out

That this was just a friendly game of cards
And nothing to get worked up about.
But McCormack would not be pacified.
Rising from his table and turning away,
He said, 'Rules are rules, and the man
Who cheats on one will cheat on all.'
We haven't spoken since that day.

NED McCORMACK

The bad drop in Dave Harrington
Comes from the mother's side.
'Twas there sixty years ago
When his gran'-aunt, Sile Moylan,
Despite repeated warnin's,
Stayed courtin' with a Tan.
So we shaved the blond hair
That curled the length of her back
And we painted her bald head
In the Union Jack.

And now I hear young Harrington
Plays Shylock with the poor.
Wan warnin' only he'd have got
In my time. Ignorin' that,
He'd have found himself behind a ditch,
Where we'd shoot the hoor.

ARMAGH JOHN

'*Tús maith, leath na hoibre*', the Gaelic proverb goes
(Most people here won't use a word of Gaelic),
But I got off to a rocky start
As owner of the shop they called 'Miss Eily's'
When, on my first night in Knockore,
I visited the Oh So Posh bar
And found the smug Kerrymen singing
'Sean South of Garryowen',
Their glasses raised in fervour
And their bellies full of Guinness,
All of them ready to die for Ireland
After *Match of the Day* was over.
When they heard I was from Crossmaglen,
They asked me for a song, but I declined,
So they struck up 'The Merry Ploughboy'
And 'Boolavogue'. Again they pressed me
For a ballad from the place they called
'The Bandit Country of the North';
When I again declined, they pressed me further
With cries of: 'Wan for Ireland, and the men
Who always dared to fight the fight.'
It was then I sang the song of Roger Casement
Arrested on the lonely beach at Banna
In the heartbeat of the Kingdom
By just two policemen, who escorted him,
Unchallenged by a single Kerryman,
To Tralee Jail. '*Could not one man be found,*'
The song asked, '*In all that Kingdom's ground,*
To save our man on lonely Banna Strand?

Oh never say that, in this noble land
Of Pearse and Emmet and MacBride,
And all these gallant men who died
That freedom might survive, there lives a knave
Who would stand idly by and watch the brave
Roger Casement taken to Tralee
And never strike a blow to set him free.'
'So there's your song,' I said when I had finished,
'Of men who always dared to fight the fight.'
The patriots from Knockore stood there, dumbstruck,
While I polished off my pint of Guinness
And went out into a chastened Kerry night.

CRANKY ANDY BOO

We had this joke:
The man who reaches seventy
Should never force a fart,
Pass up the opportunity to pee,
Or ignore an erection, what's that.
But on this second of November,
When McGettigan's sermon on the Holy Souls
Filled my mind with thoughts of going under,
And the gloomy winter cold
Had me hugging the fire in vain,
I stared into the flames, surmising:
There is nothing funny about being old.

FONCY ALLMAN

When I opened the envelope
And found her obituary
Red-circled in a page
From the *Sacramento Chronicle*,
And the unsigned note:
'She said, before she died, to let you know',
I sat for a long time and wept
At the pain and heartache,
All over now.
Then I trundled to that bed
And slept.

JIM THE RUBBISH MAN

No one knows for certain
Who fathered Mickeleen Dan,
For his mother, Cara Evans,
Is your discreet woman,

But 'tis noticed in the village
This past year or more
That she's switched to doin' her shoppin'
In Moss Hanley's Corner Store
And he's sellin' babies' nappies,
Which he never did before.

And also 'tis established
She can purchase on the slate
And he'll never reprimand her
If the settlement runs late.

Moss Hanley is the father,
Says Cranky Andy Boo,
And his guilty-conscience actions
Prove that this is so.

But what men do seems different
In the eyes of different men:
There's talk of Hanley's charity
From Charles McGettigan.

NORA HANSON

Luck follows luck, they say,
And no sooner had the Widow Connor's sons
Landed their two fine jobs
Than she won a thousand pounds
In a raffle for the Knockore GAA
I was happy for my closest friend,
Knowin' the years of struggle
She'd come through, and all the times
Her childer hadn't bit nor sup.
Want, it was, brought us together,
For just about the time her Tommy died,
My man took to drink,
And my care, too, often went without,
While the money for the bite to ate
Flowed down their father's gullet.
If things improved for wan of us
We'd never see the other short:
She has a sister in America
Who sends her clothes; she'd give me a share
Of the parcel when it came.
And the odd time himself went on the dry,
I'd bake the extra loaf of bread.
And so we managed to get by.

Wan thing only bothered me —
The way that money has
Of travellin' to a person's head.
Just look what happened to Miss Eily Shea,
A woman that grew richer by the day

But all the time went back into herself,
Preferrin' her own company,
Even in the winter nights,
So that no one ever knew
About the swanky furniture she kept
Until her door was opened for her wake.
There she was, laid out
In her palace of a sittin' room,
With fancy pictures hangin' on the walls
And polished silver on display,
And even the hallway
Drippin' with the power of money.
I couldn't help remarkin' it was sad
That no one saw her lovely house
Till she was dead.

She landed in the door
And placed five hundred in my hand.
'I have no need of this,' she said,
'What with the two boys earnin'
And steady money comin' in,
But can't the whole world see
Himself is on a heavy batter now
And you must find it extra tough
To make ends meet.
So take it – will you take it, I say –
And preten' nothin'. No one knows,
And no one needs to know.
And for God's sake never tell himself
Or he'll have it drunk before the night is out.
I'm surprised at you, Nora,

Sheddin' tears so easy;
Haven't the two of us learned by now
That cryin' is a waste of time,
Although I'll grant
You got it harder than myself.
For me at least there's sympathy
And talk about the cruelty of life
That swept a good man from me in his prime,
But how often will you hear the understandin' word
For a poor drunkard's wife.
Only it's time she made him
Pull himself together
Instead o' being too soft on him.'

With that she was gone,
Leavin' me there starin'
At the money in my hand
And thinkin' that she'd never know
The hole she got me out of this time,
And that when things were comin' sore
Only a fool would settle on Pill Hill
When Cows Lane is the grandest place to live
In all Knockore.

NORA HANSON

Oh little fella in the crib,
Thanks.

VERA HALPIN

Go out, child, to the garden
And gather a bunch of rhubarb,
And run down with it to Betts Molloy's
And carry a head of lettuce, as you're at it,
And, for the life of you,
Take no money from her,
Not even a penny for yourself
To buy bull's eyes,
The way she'll feel obliged to bake us
Wan of her lovely pies.

Jimmy Hanson

Now, in the clear light of day,
And stone-cold sober
(But not for long, I hear Nora
Sarcastically say),

And with all the sincerity I can muster,
My hand firmly on my heart,
And having no recourse
To any alcoholic bluster –

And though those Dublin doctors,
To whom I was persuaded to go
In a moment of weakness,
Would have me to know

And would press me to admit
Otherwise –
I hereby openly assert:
Drink does not control me,
I control it.

Only on a night like tonight
When I'm drunk to my total satisfaction
(I wonder where she got that twenty quid
I found in her purse today?)
And the thirst in my blood
Is, for now,
Wonderfully sated, in a way
I manage only once in a blue moon,

And my head hits the pillow
Like a cement block,
And I'm half aware of Nora
Standing over me,
Thanking whoever it is
Has brought me home to bed
(Worry on her face
As she asks him, is there any chance
I might choke on my own vomit) –
Only on such a night,
And even then only for one
Brief moment before
I drift into unconsciousness,
I see myself
With a wounding, devastating clarity
Denied to sober fools
And I say to myself:
Jimmy, you're sloshed and you're happy,
But you're also a ravin' alcoholic
And the booze
Has you completely and absolutely
Licked.

Praised be the water of life!
Our guiding light! Our shining star!
Praised be its kick in the blood!

Cursed be the way it leads us
To what we are.

Nora Hanson

Isn't it great, the way,
When he's loaded up with whiskey,
He'll talk about seeing himself for what he is,
And promise to go back again
To the doctors he cursed
Not too long ago.

I must have married him because
He reminds me of my own father,
Who is ten stone overweight,
And who makes the solemn declaration
That he'd badly need to go on a diet,
Every day
After dinner
When his belly is too full.

JOHN THE DUCKER

Wan daycent man is Jimmy Hanson.
The shirt off his own back he'd give,
If only he had it,
And yesterday he had.

I was waitin' at the door
Of the Oh So Posh
Prompt at openin' time,
When he arrived, burstin' for the cure.
He escorted me within, and without any fuss
Put a twenty-pound note on the table.
Then he ordered whiskey for the both of us.

He's your daycent hoor!

Sometime later, when the shakes were gone,
He said he'd chance a fiver on the ponies.
The horse came in at twelve to wan.

From that till closin' time,
When Stephen Holly took him home,
We had a mighty session.

My hat off to Hanson:
He even gave the barman a tip.

He don't have it often,
But when he do,
No better man to let it rip.

JIMMY HANSON

Good Friday.
Three o'clock.
Not a sinner to be seen
In all of Main Street and Cows Lane.

Knockore Church is burstin' at the seams
And McGettigan's sermon
Is sombre and deliberate.

Not that I am there to hear it.

Nineteen hours yet
Before the pubs will open.

Myself and John the Ducker
Stand at the Corner in the pourin' rain
Tryin' hard to think
Of a way to get McGuire to let us in.

Charlie's Angel, in a hurry, passes by.
'Are ye not goin' to church?' she asks.

We don't bother to reply.

Here, in the main street of Knockore,
As the rain sheets down and the sky darkens,
We thirst until our tongues are sore.

And all our bones are tremblin'
With the shakes.

Good Friday in the rain,
And nineteen hours to go:
Enough to make the heart sink.
Water, water everywhere.

And not a drop to drink.

Dan McGuire (Publican)

Who'd own a pub?

Two days in the year,
Today and Christmas Day,
We have for wife and family,
And will they let us have them in peace?
No fear!

I peep out through the curtains;
They're still there,
Hoppin' from one leg to the other,
Lookin', for all the world, like a pair
Of schoolboys that can't wait to pee.

Wouldn't you think they'd go home out o' the rain?

I'll set herself on 'em
If they knock on my door again.

Two days in the year
For wife and family
And all they can think
Of is the drink.

AMY THE DUCKER

Gone again
When I come in!
And without my permission!
Gone drinkin'!
If I catch him
I'll kill him, I'll kill him, I'll kill him!
I'll let him see
He's not playin' with Nora Hanson.

John the Ducker

Two great misfortunes in my life.

The first, a shrew of a wife
Who won't let me leave the house
To have my drink in peace,
So that I have to sneak out,
Quiet as a mouse,
The minute her back is turned.

The second, this curse of a nickname.

When she'd come after me,
Seekin' me out in the Oh So Posh,
I'd have men on guard within,
Drinkin' by the window,
And when they'd see her comin',
That mouth of hers tight with temper,
And the quickness of her stride
Declarin' to all and sundry
That she was bent on murder,
They'd shout their timely warnin':
'Quick, John! Duck her! Duck her!'
And that was the savin' signal
To send me quickly scurryin'
Into my secret cubbyhole,
Where I'd remain in silence
Until the danger passed.

And so it came about
That I was called John the Duck Her,
A name I was rightly proud of,
Because it told the story
Of my heroic struggle
With that wicked shrew of a woman,
Who, despite her threats and schemin',
Couldn't keep me from the drink.

But somehow or another,
The name was lost in transit,
And I was left with a handle
That is nothin' short of insultin',
Suggestin', as it does,
That I'm the type who dodges
Every lawful activity
That life might throw at me.

There are days when I feel like screamin',
'My name is not John the Ducker –
It's John the Duck Her.
And don't forget to pronounce the 'h'
Before the last 'er'.

JIM THE RUBBISH MAN

Since knee-high to a grasshopper, I could not be bested
At solving jigsaws, and that is why
Torn bits of documents in rubbish bins
Are an open challenge to my expertise.

Ever since poor Mike Dunne
(Some names I don't mind naming)
Lost, first, the wife to cancer
And, shortly afterwards, his only son
To some disease with a long name
Above in a Dublin hospital,
He's turned in on himself.
The seldom times he walks the streets,
He talks to no one,
Nor has a living soul
Darkened the inside of his house
Since the day his son was planted.
Above all, the man grew mean.
He passes by church-gate collections,
Growls from his door at the ticket-selling children
And won't reward the music of the Wren.
He's even gone too mean to feed himself,
And what used to be a beefy mountain of a man
Has fallen away to nothin'.

Imagine my surprise
When the torn scraps of paper,
At last put properly together, as only I could do,
On the greasy surface of my kitchen table,

Spelt: 'Dear Mr Dunne
Our Lady's Hospital for Sick Children, Crumlin,
Wishes to acknowledge
Your latest contribution of one thousand pounds.
Thank you for your continuing generosity.'

EILEEN LEE

Which of my four flowers do I love best?
Is it Kieran, my young daisy,
Whose sunny smile
Is always edged with mischief?

Or Maura, my red-haired rose –
A bit thorny, but worth the effort,
And so beautiful you'd stop to look?

Or Deirdre, the snowdrop,
Who is sickly and pale,
But strong of character,
Like the first flower of winter
That won't shirk the challenge
Of wind and weather?

Or Siobhán, my eldest,
My golden daffodil,
Long and willowy
And there when most wanted,
A sure sign of spring
After a trying winter?

Which flower do I love best?
I love them all, though one I love
Dearer than all the rest.
She is Sarah, my water lily,
Who was always that bit distant,
And hard to come close to.

But one evening last May
She was drowned in the Shannon,
And now the more I love her
The more my heart is breaking.
Oh God of giving and taking,
I ask you yet again:
Break the nightmare cycle
Of pain feeding on love
And love feeding on pain.

And who says they bring more tears than joy?
One sparkling moment makes worthwhile
All the care and worry.

Kieran came to me just now,
Whimpering.
He'd scratched his left eye,
So it was weeping.
I kissed it gently and consoled:
'It'll soon be better, pet.'

A minute later he was back again
And, covering his right eye,
He looked up and asked,
'Mum, does it see you yet?'

FINBARR O'KEEFFE

Is it because I am from Cork
That, even after twenty-seven years,
Something is still withheld,
If only for that crucial hour
On Munster Final day
When the Blood and Bandage
Meets the Green and Gold
And a rivalry,
Irreconcilable as clashing colours,
Old as the county bounds,
Recurring as the second Sunday in July,
Shutters the hearts
Of the sunniest people under God's sky?

Result and Consequence

Kerry have been beaten!
Shock! Disbelief!
And now we'll have to listen
To Finbarr O'Keeffe.

Vincent Power

Did you ever hear such baloney
As spouted last night in the Oh So Posh
From the ignorant mouth of Tim Danagher
When the talk turned to football
And I tried to convince him –
In the most reasonable way –
That the giants of my time
Were ten times better than the boys of today?

'No sissies back then,'
I assured him, 'but hardened men
Who'd only leave the battlefield
If they were on their last breath,
Or a broken limb or a burst vessel
Had 'em close to death.

And there was no whistlin' by the referee
For every tittle-tattle;
You'd have to be half killed
Before you'd earn your free.'

He wasn't a bit impressed by me.
'From listenin' to you,' he said,
'I think I'd be safe in assumin'
'Twas kick-boxin', not football, ye played.
And all your arguments were settled
Not by class or skill
But with brute force, and fightin',
And movin' in for the kill.'

Wasn't that nice talk, now, from an upstart young brat
Who wouldn't lace my boots when I was in my prime!

Give me back forty years
And I'd stretch him flat.

Bosco Collins (Selector)

1

I'd go out of my mind
If I'd Nell Hogan for a mother:
'Don't pick my Pateen,' she wails,
'My Pateen is too refined.'

2

Take no notice of Tim Danagher
If he leaves the field
Covered with blood.

He can make his nose bleed
And he'll smear himself
And cry to be brought off
If his marker is too good.

3

Every man is entitled to wan mistake,
And Mosheen Dowd,
A fine full-back in his time,
Made his the night
He made Mosheen Óg.

4

Watch Ben McCartan when he hits someone;
He'll fall to the ground himself
And cry out in pain.
The ref will never know
Who struck the first blow.

5

Pats Dolan let us down again.
A clinker with the dry ball,
Hopeless in the rain.

6

Would you ever think that Ger Foley,
The man who wasn't afraid to tame
Mike Moran's bull,
Is a bag of nerves
And spends twenty minutes pukin'
Before every game?

7

Do you remember the great fight
That started after the game
With the Gale Rangers
Above in their parish hall
When the two teams were toggin' off
And Foley, naked as a baby,
Climbed on a table and said
He was ready to be strung
Up for the murder of the first Gale man
Who climbed up on the table with him
And wan of their women who ran in
On hearing the commotion
Looked up at Foley in admiration and sung
His praises with the remark:
'Aren't the Knockore lads well hung?'

8

If ye want Sergeant Marron not to raid the pub
After closin' time on the night of the match,
Tell his useless son to bring on his boots
And write him down as fifth sub.

9

Nedeen Donlan would need more
Than sickness pills to travel.
He'll bate any man alive
In our own football field.
But take him out o' Knockore
And you'll see the head go down
And the shoulders shrug.
Away from his home patch,
Nedeen wouldn't bate snow off a rug.

10

You'd think you'd be made by Phil Hannigan:
No better fielder of the ball,
No speedier wing-forward
To leave his man behind.
But wait until
You see the crooked kick:
The man wouldn't point a pencil.

11

To pick or to drop Simon Dee?
He won't burn a ball in play,
But no matter what the angle,
He'll score from the close-in free.

12

The unluckiest man by far
In the whole of Knockore is Paul Carter.
How many times, I ask myself,
Has he struck the crossbar?

13

I was stuck for a right corner-forward,
So, happenin' to meet Marron on the street, I consulted
Him. He thought long and hard
Before saying, 'Isn't it funny now,
But I'd play my own son there.'
'Isn't it damn funny,' says I.
Would you believe the man was insulted?

14

At the Knockore GAA social,
The pensioner, Sam Hall,
Argued for most of an hour
With his former team-mate, Clive Dunne,
About a pass he claims he should have got
In the final of '51.
They had to be separated when
Things were inclined to get a bit sour.

15

When all is said and done,
I think the best man for the corner-forward job
Is my own son.

16

The five subs?
God help us.
If Jacky Con Donal
Can make the first fifteen,
Where does that leave
The five subs?

17

The only wan I'd hold out hope for
Is Weedy McStay.
He has class to burn
But can't put on the weight.
They say 'tis the women
Have him wore away.

18

With the legs he has, Nicky McBride
Would be better off waltzin'.
The legs he brought from the mother's side.

19

Ye can bring on Dame Margot,
But only if the game is won
With five minutes to go.
When he starts on his solo run
To nowhere,
Prancin' like a ballerina,
They'll laugh and clap him loud;
Dame Margot should only be brought on
To entertain the crowd.

20

Go on, now,
Answer fair and square:
Sure the black and red of the Gale
Don't look half as nice
As the blue and white of Knockore?

Mickeen:
You'll be on their county man –
A farmer like yourself, Mickeen,
And, we hear, as nice a man as you could meet,
And most obligin' in his daily life.
You haven't a hope in hell
Of stayin' with him, Mickeen,
For he's lightnin' fast,
But for us to have a chance at all,
He must be kep' reasonably quiet.
To counteract his threat, I have devised a plan:
You must talk to him, Mickeen.
You must talk to him in all sincerity.
Tell him you're a settled, married man,
With the wife expectin' any day,
But that you're driven to near-despair
With sickness on the land.
Ask him have he any cure
For red water and the scour.
Tell him that you're findin' it
Impossible to cope
With these and sundry other plagues;
Ask for his advice, Mickeen,
Ask for it in all sincerity.
Tell him he's your last hope
Of keepin' the roof over your head,
And that if he don't come up with somethin' fast,
House, farm and all will go
And you'll be thrown out on the roadside –

You and your expectant wife –
And would he like
To have that on his conscience
For the rest of his life.
Get him focused, Mickeen,
On matters elsewhere
By appealin' to his better nature
And bit by bit
Slow things down
To walkin'
Pace.
He won't notice it
If you can get him
Talkin', talkin', talkin'.

BOSCO COLLINS

If God made anything nicer than sex,
It has to be the feelin' I got
When the long whistle sounded
In the final of the North Kerry Championship
And Knockore had buried without trace
The boyos from the Gale.

The long whistle!
The mighty cheer!
The sweet sound of victory!

If God made anything nicer than *that*,
He kep' it for Himself.

GREG HOARE

On the phone to Paul Canavan,
Top heart specialist at St Mary's Hospital,
We joked about the Final of '64,
When the Gale hammered Knockore
And he broke my nose
With a sneaky, dirty elbow.
We argued again about that incident
As if it happened yesterday.
Then I told him of my sister
Who was in urgent need of a bypass.
Canavan put her top of his list
And operated straightaway.

ELEANOR FOLEY

Don't for a minute believe
All that nonsense about
The winnin' of the cup goin' to my head.

True, not a word had passed between us
For the ten months since
His foray up Miss Eily's Lane
(And don't remind me of that again)
But by now anyone could see
The man was truly sorry –
He'd even let his appearance go
To rack and ruin –
So that 'twas only a matter of time
Before I'd come round anyway
To thinkin' I should
Let bygones be bygones.

Then, when I saw the team paradin'
Down Main Street,
And the Knockore Pipe Band
Playin' all that lovely music,
And Bosco Collins, at their head,
Cryin' like a baby as he waved the cup,
And himself glum as ever
Despite all the celebratin',
My heart began to soften.

And when I saw 'em makin' for the Oh So Posh,
I says to myself: Eleanor,
You can stay here sulkin' forever
With your gloomy man
Or the pair o' ye can go out
For wan whale of a night
Of singin' and dancin' and carousin',
To celebrate the winnin' of the cup.

So I turns to him and says,
'Pat, I think it's time we made it up.'

MARIANNE CROWLEY

Talk of a night when the cup
Was brought home to Knockore!

It lasted the twelve weeks
From December the first
Until Ash Wednesday.

Himself and myself stuck the pace
Until January nineteen.
That night, home late as usual,
We were met at the front door
By our sixteen-year-old, Eileen,
Who said we were an absolute disgrace.

Now we need her permission
If we're to go celebratin' any more.

TOM COPSE

On holiday in Ireland
In Olympic year, 2000,
I was anxious to see
How my fellow Americans would do
In the finals of the track-and-field events.
As chance would have it, I was passing through
A sleepy little village named Knockore.
I stopped at a dingy pub,
Ridiculously called the Oh So Posh,
To view the games on television
And was rather surprised to find
The place was empty.
'Say, proprietor,' I enquired,
'How come there's nobody here to watch
The Olympics?' 'Unfortunately, sir,'
Came the reply, 'they're clashing
With the first round of the parish league
And all my customers are gone to the match.'

TARA TRAVERS

Let me compose a prophecy,
Seeing that I've nothing else to do
On this sunny day of June
In 1952,
As I wait, impatiently,
For the winter cold and rain
That will drive the children
Back into my room again,
Where they'll sit on the floor
In front of a cosy fire
And listen to my stories
Of Helen of Troy,
Of Priam and Hecuba,
Of Icarus and Daedalus,
And many, many more.

Sometime, at the turn of the century,
Someone, somewhere will ask you
This simple question:
Why do you love Knockore?

And you will answer:
It is because once upon a time,
So long ago I'm not even sure
If the whole thing isn't a dream,
There was a woman dressed in smelly black,
Talking in a battered chair,
Breaking her story only now and then
To reach for the tongs

I never could quite manage,
To feed or rearrange the fire
That sent smoke curling slowly upwards,
Where it formed in the dim air
Figures of Priam and Hecuba and the fair
Helen of Troy,
And listening to her every word
Was an enchanted boy
Who was, I think, even then, vaguely aware
That this woman and her village
Bestowed a special privilege.

QUESTION

Where in the Oh So Posh will you find
The man who can't talk the leg off a pot?
Answer:
You will not.

THE OH SO POSH

1

Some nights ago – as usual – there came
To me a motley group of twelve or so
Knockorians. Did I say motley?
I mean that only in the sense
Of an apparent lack of purpose underlying
This haphazard meeting,
Of which there are no minutes,
For which there was no set agenda,
Unless, of course, one understands
That any topic might be raised,
Granted only its potential
To stimulate discussion of the type
That fosters a roguish brotherhood
And sends men home at an ungodly hour
In tune with others and themselves.

After the initial pleasantries,
The conversation turned first
To the impending retirement
Of Séamus Mac An tSionnaigh,
Headmaster of the local national school for forty years,
And this, in turn, led to reminiscences,
Especially of the humorous kind,
As, for example, the old master's habit
Of saying 'Day gone – nothing done'
Each afternoon when the clock struck one.
There was talk, too, of his happy style
Of teaching, and how he never used the cane

For anything except answers to the Catechism,
The which, he said,
'Should be beaten into every child
Before temptation rears its ugly head.'
'And right he was,' said Bosco Collins, 'for to this day,
There's not a question in the Catechism
That I can't answer.' Needless to say,
Collins was tested on this:
When is a sin mortal?
What is forbidden by the Sixth and Ninth?
What are the precepts of the Church?
When is contrition perfect?
And here there was a long digression,
Lasting some three pints or more,
When Joey Hourigan maintained there were
Sins it was impossible to be sorry for.
He cited, to advance his argument,
His first night as an exile in New York,
When he was just a boy of seventeen
And 'This big black mama took me home
And introduced me to the art
Of making love. That was October first, 1983,
But she had me thinking it was my birthday.
I often ask myself since then,
In times of crisis and especially when
I'm going to Confession,
If I'm really sorry for that sin.'
'For one as well up in the Catechism as me,'
Said Bosco Collins, 'it's plain to see
That, provided you're afraid of hell
Or losin' out on heaven, you're dead safe.

That's what imperfect sorrow is about.'
With one man's conscience finally at peace,
The theological discussion
Turned suddenly bawdy,
With each man in the company
Invited to tell about the sin
He found it hardest to be sorry for.
Then, were you to believe the words
That issued from each lubricated throat,
No Sodom or Gomorrah
Would touch Knockore
For skulduggery of every kind,
But most especially for fornication
And the gleeful taking of a cute revenge.
May I, however, make this observation,
As one who has played host
To many gatherings like this:
It is a foible of Knockorians
That when well-oiled,
They lapse into a wild exaggeration
In order to acquire a reputation
Only to be forged in hell,
As though, suddenly, they have tired
Of the unrelenting caution
Which is the hallmark of their sober lives,
As though the good name they guard
With an aggressive jealousy
Has now become a worthless thing.
And so it might be prudent to dismiss
These tales of lusty conquests, and such like,
As fabrications of a mind

Revolting at the daily grind.
Let us come to when these tales are over,
To Bosco Collins and his Catechism
And some further testing of his memory:
What happened on Pentecost Sunday?
What is the mystery of the Incarnation?
How do we show our love for our neighbour?
Mention of 'neighbour' turned the talk
To Armagh John, the new man in Knockore.
While some were feeling still a little sore
At his outrageous song of Roger Casement,
All were agreed the man should get
A proper welcome to the Kingdom,
'And all the more especially
Since we gave 'em such a hammerin'
In 1953.'
So then and there a plot was hatched
To give the exile from the North
A proper Kingdom welcome –
Yet one to let him know
Knockorians should never be dismissed
With songs of Roger Casement and the like.
The plotting lasted well into the night –
Way beyond closing time, until a guard arrived,
And thereupon my premises were cleared.

2
Last night, as usual, they came again
And, though a storm raged and rain
Poured down, great was the glee
And free the conversation

135

As they discussed at length
The successful execution of their plan
Which, if what they said was true,
Was implemented thus:

Armagh John, by this time, was notorious
As a temperate and regular man
Who drank only in small doses –
Never beyond four pints – and then
Only on Tuesday nights
When there was a game of Forty-one.
As pre-arranged, however, on last Tuesday night,
Some *poitín* was slyly dropped into his porter
And, as time wore on, he found himself
Growing extremely happy, and prepared to stay
Much longer than usual.

Meanwhile, not far away,
Our boys employed the help of Mickeen Connor,
A nifty youngster, very promising
At football, if he only grew.
They approached Miss Eily's grocery from the rear,
Where there was a tiny window.
This they forced, and lifted in Mickeen,
Who landed like a sparrow on the floor
And in a wink had opened the front door
To others waiting on the street outside.
Bosco Collins – all prepared – was there.
He'd brought along his ass and car,
The wheels of which were soon dismantled,
Allowing the body of the car pass through

The open door. It barely fitted
But once inside, the wheels were reattached.
The donkey was brought in
And tackled to the car and then,
With everything in order,
The door was closed again.

Straight on the dot of closing time,
Each patron floored his pint
And left my premises.
Armagh John left too, his spirits high,
And fortified with dollops of *poitín*;
To crown it all he'd won
A chicken at the game of Forty-one.
So, feeling quite magnanimous, he declared
That even though all Kerrymen were cowards,
Knockorians weren't the worst. He reached his door
And turned the key – and there, before
His startled gaze, was Bosco's ass and car.
Around his neck the donkey wore
A placard reading: 'Welcome to Knockore'.
'I must be seeing things,' said John.
So, closing the door behind him, he
Walked out again, and then re-entered,
Expecting to find the vision gone,
But no such luck. Facing him still,
With drooping tail and with indifferent stare,
Was Bosco's donkey, tackled to the car.
Again Armagh John rushed out
Into the street and gave a shout
For help. From nowhere, then, it seemed,

Knockorians emerged, asking what was wrong.
And on beholding Bosco's donkey there,
They scratched their polls almightily,
As if completely baffled.
'How in God's name did *he* get in?'
Asked Joey Hourigan, pointing to the ass.
'By all the laws of trigonometry
And meeting at a certain point,
No car this size could ever pass
Through this front door. You could well
Believe it is some sort of miracle.'
'Will ye try to get him out?'
Pleaded John, and, being as ever keen
To help a neighbour in distress,
The men from Knockore did their level best.
The ass was untackled; then
They stood the car on either side
And upside down and downside up;
They tried from front and from behind –
But all in vain.
''Tis no use, lads,' said Bosco. 'Ye might as well
Be trying to piss against the wind.
It looks as if this car is here to stay.'
Poor Armagh John slumped in dismay.
'What will I do in the morning?' he wailed.
'Won't all my customers take flight
When they see this apparition here
Before them?' Then out stepped Andy Boo.
'I know how,' he said,
'To get the car out of here, nice
And handy. But there's a price

To pay for such intelligence.'
'And what might that price be?' asked Bosco
With childlike innocence. 'Well,' said Boo, 'before
Donkey and car will leave this shop,
Our Northern friend must sing
Three verses of "The Sash My Father Wore".'
Every Knockorian, fair do's to him,
Angrily protested then
That this was a lousy way to take advantage
Of a businessman's predicament.
'Surely to God,' they said,
'We can do better for this poor misfortunate
Who, as things stand, could see his livelihood
Swept from under his feet, come mornin'.'
But Andy Boo was adamant:
'The ass and car stays here as long
As it takes Caruso to sing the song.'
The Northerner was outraged. 'I'd rather be dead
Than sing that song,' he said.
Then John the Ducker, an experienced arbitrator
At marts and fair days and such like,
Went to and fro between the opposing parties
Until at last it was agreed
That for just two verses of 'The Sash'
Andy would help this grocer
In his desperate hour of need.
And so it was that Armagh John
Opened his mouth full throttle
And sang 'The Sash' as tunefully
As ever you'd hear down Shankill way
On a sunny Twelfth of July.

It chanced that Alan Glynn had brought along
His tape recorder, and every note
That issued from the throat
Of that fine singer was then played back to him.
'We understand you come from Crossmaglen,'
Said Andy Boo. 'Well, now, let me tell you
That if we ever hear another verse
About Casement and his accident in Banna,
We'll send this tape up North,
Complete with a photo of yourself
Above the caption: "Kerry Convert to the Orange Cause".
And, for your homework, you must learn the song
About the boys who died in Gortagleanna,
So that whenever you are asked to sing again
You'll praise the deeds of these brave Kerrymen.'
Bosco Collins spoke up next. 'Armagh John
Is a credit to his county,' he said, 'and now
'Tis time we carried out our side of the bargain.'
They set to work, and before long
Donkey and car were back outside again.
'And finally,' said Andy Boo to John,
'So that you'd know we really do
Welcome you to Kerry, we've brought along
Young Mickeen Connor. Recently he got
A bugle for a birthday present
And he's been practisin' a lot.'
Mickeen was led in, a trumpet in his hand.
'We want you, lad,' said Andy,
'To play "A Nation Once Again"
For this fervent patriot from Crossmaglen,
And every last man here will sing along.'

There was, unfortunately, one hitch:
This song was not in Mickeen's repertoire.
In fact, there was just one tune he could play –
A doleful version of 'Oh Mein Papa'.
''Twill have to do,' said Joey Hourigan.
'Strike up the note, Mickeen,
And wance we get the start we'll all join in.'
Young Mickeen played. 'Let every man
Sing now as best he can,'
Said Joey, and indeed they did,
Their voices carrying through the midnight air:
'*Oh mein Papa,*
To me you are so wonderful.
Oh mein Papa
To me you are so good.
Gone are the days
When he would take me on his knee . . . '
Now, whether it was the doleful melody
Or the warmth of that Knockorian welcome
Or, maybe, the effects of the *poitín,*
Poor Armagh John broke down in tears.
'What's wrong?' asked Andy.
'It's just that, though he's dead for twenty years,
The song has put me thinkin' of my dad.
But then again, your lovely welcome
Has raised the cockles of my heart
So that I don't know if I'm crying
Because I am too happy or too sad.'
Armagh John and Cranky Andy Boo
Hugged one another, and Andy, too,
Began to cry. 'That bloody tune

Would draw a tear from a stone,'
He whimpered between sobs.
Then, when the song was ended, each man there
Wished Armagh John once more
The happiest of welcomes to Knockore;
They slapped his back, and shook
His hand in friendship.
Then, happy at a job well done,
They said goodbye and headed off for home.

Tonight, as usual, they'll come again,
A motley group of twelve or so
Knockorians . . .

Sis Kerrigan

Ask the people of Knockore
How they regard Sis Kerrigan:
The bane of many marriages,
A temptress among men,
They'll say to you –
And that is true.

She married Ivor Gantley,
Loaded down with cash
But ugly as you'd wish to see.
She married him for money
Not for love, they'll say to you –
And that is true.

How he endured her ways,
Her drinking and carousing,
Her open infidelities,
God alone knows.

Only contempt and ridicule
Did she extend to him,
Only the spending of his wealth,
Only the slow and stealthy
Saddening of his character
For thirty years or so –
All this they know.

Then ask them how they view
That accident

Which, when he was sixty-two,
Crushed his mind and body;
They will talk of the grim
Irony that meant
She must now care for him.

She must care for him
In everything.
She must care for him
In toiletry and dress;
But look, as she takes his arm
To fit into a sleeve,
See how tenderly she guides him.
And that rubbing, kind and warm –
Is that a caress?

A thousand times at night he calls her name,
'Sis, Sis, Sis, Sis, Sis' –
Persistent as the drip of rain.
A thousand times she rises
To turn him in bed,
Then, on his cold, damp forehead,
A thousand times she plants a kiss.

Nor will he eat unless
Hers be the hand
That spoons each morsel to his mouth.
It is a hand that seems to bless.
And when each meal is through,
He smiles – as though he understands
Her whispered 'I love you'.

CRANKY ANDY BOO

Don't make me laugh with all this talk
Of how Sis Kerrigan has changed.
This is the wan, remember,
Who, in her youth and bloom,
Bedded all around her,
Left, right and centre,
Every man she could find.
And now you expect me to believe
That she has grown – how's that you put it? –
All wise and caring.
Take it from me, she's still
The same oul' Kerrigan,
And there's been no miraculous
Conversion to report.
All that's happened is that the rage
In her blood has cooled,
Just as befell the rest of us
When the passing years and old age
Took their toll. The truth
Is that if you could only lubricate
Her veins with some of the magic oil
From the fountain of youth,
She'd be just as fired up and randy
As ever she was. Wise, is it you say?
Wise is only another way
For saying she's gone off the boil.

Joey Hourigan

David Harrington was killed
In that accident
Which left Ivor Gantley mindless and broken.
His wife, shocked and tearless,
Sat by the coffin, while we queued
In a long line to offer her
Our 'Sorry for your troubles, ma'am'.
David Junior cried
Inconsolably and loud
And his listening classmates
Felt an unaccustomed fear
At seeing their friend
Behave so out-of-character.

Afterwards, in a crowded Oh So Posh –
Crowded but subdued –
We tried to make sense of it.

'We do be pushin' and shovin',,'
Observed Bosco Collins,
'Instead o' mindin' our prayers.
And every so often the Man Above
Do have to send a warnin'.'

And many nodded in agreement.

'We do be too fond of the money, if you ask me,'
Said Paddy Dee,
'And thinkin' there's a pocket in the habit

Instead o' payin' attention
To what McGettigan has to say.'

Mac An tSionnaigh spoke
Of the cruel uncertainty of life
And – maybe it was the teacher in him –
Began to sermonise about the need
Always to be prepared to meet our Maker.

He put the fear o' God in us.

And, as the night wore on,
We grew morose and gloomy,
And hurting with the sense
Of an angry Judge
Who might, suddenly and without warnin',
Call any one of us to face Him
In the witness box.

Nor did we get one trace
Of comfort from the Pagan Cummings
When he once again pronounced:
'There cannot be a God. There is no God.'

He was the gloomiest man in all the place.

Andy Boo

Don't Grace Harrington look well, Bosco,
Beside her stretched-out man?
And can't you see the cut of the wealth
In that necklace she has on?
A lovely-lookin' woman
In the whole of her health,
And money to go with it!
There'll be no shortage of men
Ready to chance their luck when
The time of mournin' is done.
There's more mileage in her, I tell you.
'Twon't be too long at all before
She'll be up and motorin' again.

Alan Glynn

This journalist came from the papers.
He asked – and I explained –
How the accident took place;
And all the time I was talkin',
He called me 'Mr Glynn',
He nodded his head with grave assent
At everything I said,
And he scribbled at a mighty pace.
He had me thinkin'
I was an important man.

Then, all of a slap, he hits me with:
'Off the record, Mr Glynn,
What kind of thug
Was David Harrington?'
I wouldn't know much about him,' I lied.

'There are stories doing the rounds,'
My scribbler ferreted.
'I'd know nothin' about them,' I said.
'He was a distant class of man, you see,
As anyone in Knockore will verify.
He kept to himself
And minded his own business.
Never flattered the livin',
Never spoke ill of the dead.
The world might be a better place
If we all did the same,' I said.

Bosco Collins

When Roundy Mulherne died,
Aged one hundred and four,
Peteen Duignan remembered
He had fielded for Knockore
Back in the 1920s.
So we formed our guard of honour
At either side of the hearse
With our blue-and-white armbands
And escorted him to his grave.

After the burial we adjourned to the Oh So Posh,
Where Peteen spoke of Mulherne's deeds
On the field of play:
'No better wing-back
To meet a ball at speed and run with it
And set up an attack deep in the enemy's half.
No more stylish man in his day.'

But later that night,
When the whiskey went to his head,
Peteen softened his praise:
'True, Mulherne was a mighty man
To win a ball,' he said,
'But where was the good in that when
He couldn't kick it pissin'-distance?
And while there should be no interference
With the good name of the dead,
For the sake of truth I should state
There was no relief in his clearance.'

THE PAGAN (ADRIAN) CUMMINGS

'McGettigan,' I said,
'I'm proud to be numbered among the one per cent
Of think-for-yourself Knockorians
Who'll have no truck with a church
That scares the livin' daylights
Out of ordinary decent men and women
With all this terrifying blather
About eternal damnation.
Guilt and fear, fear and guilt
Are your tools of trade.
I wonder if you've ever even considered
The absurdity of what you preach:
On the one hand a God of infinite mercy,
On the other a Judge who would,
For a crime committed by a finite mind,
Condemn to an infinity in hell
Amid, as your theologians would have it,
Eternal flames.
All I say is, if that's what you mean by mercy,
You're more than welcome to it.
As for myself, I have my enemies,
And I've met some bastards in my time –
Men who glory in another man's misfortune –
But there's not one of them I'd hate so much
As to consign him to the type of punishment
So favoured by your God.
Honestly, it makes my blood boil . . . '

'Hold it!' McGettigan said. 'You'd do well
To remember that someone like you,
Free of the hatred you describe,
Hasn't a snowball's chance
Of ending up in hell.'

CHARLES McGETTIGAN

'On reflection, Adrian,' I said,
'That may be too facile and too glib.
So let me say this to you:
The phrase most often used in the Good Book
Is "Do not be afraid."
Three hundred and sixty-five times,
Once for each day in the year,
He puts those words before us,
As though inviting us
To a daily celebration.
Do not be afraid, He says,
Accept your fallen state and then
Accept the love you never could deserve.
The news is good, Adrian,
Enough to make us happy and be glad,
So put those thoughts of hell away
And do not be afraid.'

Afterwards, walking home,
I pray to my favourite saint,
Matthew the Evangelist,
Whose greatest pleasure was
In bringing the Good News
To those who hadn't heard.

Reaching my front door,
I grope for the keyhole
In the dim light.
Now the light is always dim

And growing dimmer still
And rapidly more dim.
Soon, and very soon, the doctor says,
There will be total darkness.
Soon I will not celebrate the Eucharist,
Or minister to a fearful soul;
Soon I must depend on those
Who would depend on me.

In my twilight sitting room,
Not bothering – for where's the point –
To turn the switch,
I slump into an armchair.
Darkness is falling fast.
Sooner or later I'll have to tell them –
Perhaps in my homily next Sunday.
Perhaps they already know.
No dimwits, my Knockorians.
Perhaps I'll get away with it
For another month or two.

Again and again I ask myself:
What will become of this blind priest?

I should have been more prudent;
There are plans I should have made.
The truth dawns as the light fades:
I am afraid.

John the Ducker

Hard to know
What to make of the new PP.

He's a daycent man, we hear,
And 'tis said that in his college days
He was a mighty scholar,
But then again,
'Tis impossible to knock a laugh out of him.
Watch him as he makes his way
Solemnly down Main Street,
So grave, so serious. How can
He be so sure that life isn't laughable
And not something that should weigh us down?
Is he, I wonder, in possession
Of some dark and gloomy secret
That has escaped the rest of us?
This isn't the first time
I've comes across an educated man
Who refuses to smile on his way through life.
Well, here's my question for all educated men:
What's all the seriousness for anyway?

If education is all about learning
The reasons why we shouldn't regard life
As sometimes, at least, bordering on farce,
You know where they can stick their learning.

Archibald Fawcett (Wyoming)

I do not understand,
I simply do not understand
This sudden, dark obsession with a place
She hardly ever mentioned
All through our long and happy marriage,
A place she never once returned to
Since leaving, half a century ago.
Till now, she seemed content
To have it purged from memory.
Year followed year
And I never heard that name.
Now, of late, it is the only thing I hear.

She should not have married me, she says;
Though she will swear
I was the only man for her.
Had I not been wed before we met
To a woman who still lives?
A union such as ours
Must, therefore, be adulterous.
Did not the priest advise the people so,
In a Sunday-morning sermon
Fifty years ago
In Knockore?

She should not have married me, she says,
Though, through her tears,
She thanks me for a happy life,
Though all these years

As my contented wife,
No priest or church had bothered her.
Now everything has changed:
She uses words she never used before;
Now there is talk from morning until night
Of church and priest and pulpit
And Knockore.

She can no longer live with me, she says.
(I listen, dumbfounded.)
She cannot live with me
Unless it be
As sister lives with brother.
She leaves my bed,
She goes into another room;
I hear her turn the key and lock the door
On her bewildered, grieving husband:
What is this church she speaks of?
Who is this priest –
Whose voice spans half a century –
From Knockore?

Knockore!
Here, in the bed she has deserted,
Baffled and reeling
From the blows you have delivered,
I ask myself:
Whatever have I done to you
That you should visit me like this?

I try to imagine you.
Are you a medieval place
Of pious superstitions,
A place where witches might still dance
Around a gruesome cauldron,
Casting a hellish trance,
As in a modern *Macbeth*?
No! Not a place, but a parasitic entity
That once upon a devilish time
Crawled from the shore
Of a land I have never visited,
Crawled into the Atlantic
And swam three thousand miles,
Then made your way,
Unbidden and insidious,
As far as Wyoming,
Till, finding a receptive host,
You lodged with us.

Nora Fawcett (Née Corridan)

Now I know why,
These past thirty years or so,
When I'd be lying
Beside him in bed, and listening
To the quiet breathing of his sleep
And thinking how lucky I was to have met him,
Suddenly I'd start to cry.

ELLA GLYNN

What a relief to be home again,
And out of that Dublin hospital,
Where a squad of specialists
Put me through all kinds of tests
Before deciding I was 'a unique case',
Even going so far as to take
Photographs of my face
For inclusion in some medical journal.
Can you imagine what it's like
To have people peering at you
So closely you can smell their breath
And see the hairs in their nostrils,
While all the time they keep asking
Questions of the most personal kind?
For the first time in my life
I was made to feel like some sort of freak.
And after all that, after a full week
Of tests and questions, all they could say
Was that they would deliberate
At length, before deciding
If or when to operate. On the first day
I went for a walk in the hospital grounds,
Only too glad to get away
From the questions and the antiseptic atmosphere,
But soon I noticed how visitors
And other patients would stop and gawk,
Enough to make me wish
I was anywhere else but where I was.
So, I didn't go out walking any more,

Just stayed in my private room, with a book.
Thank God to be back home in Knockore,
Where people accept me for what I am
And not for how I look.
Here I'm just plain Ella Glynn,
Just one more Knockorian.
Here nobody ever remarks
On my horribly disfigured face.
Here I'm taken totally for granted:
I'm part of the furniture of the place.

ÚNA TROY

Smitten by his wicked sense of fun –
Most wicked when he was drunk –
And his sharp intelligence
And his dangerous defiance of convention,
I proposed to Kevin Stapleton
On February twenty-ninth, 1964,
But he rejected me.

Though, with my auburn hair
And my hazel eyes
And my perfect features,
I was easily the prettiest in Knockore.

I cried for seven years.
Then I married Thomas Trant.

He was a steady man.

He was kind and good and hard-working
And, most of all, considerate.
I bore him seven children,
And he provided well for us
And there was not one day
In our thirty years of married life,
Until cancer swept him from me,
That he didn't show his love and gratitude.

Kevin Stapleton had married too.
He became a slave to drink.
He used to beat his wife, most viciously,
So that she shed no tears
When his jaundiced body was laid to rest.

Wasn't I the lucky woman!
And yet . . . and yet there are times
When I'm alone and reminiscing,
That I think of that wicked sense of fun
And find myself wishing . . . wishing.

Paul Roe

The truth – though I accept you won't believe it –
Is that I never really meant to stay away.

Just for a year or two, perhaps,
While that most intractable of women
Learned I was not to be trifled with.
And for the first few months, at least,
I sent some money home
To cater for our little girls, Úna and Cáit,
Though when the business opportunity arose
And finance was a top priority,
This arrangement was allowed to lapse,
Until, with one thing and another,
It was forgotten altogether.
A troubled conscience? Please understand
I really did intend returning,
And always, though my business thrived,
And wealth would bring its own temptations
And the wherewithal to self-indulge,
I never once – not once in thirty years –
Betrayed my marriage vows,
Having nothing to do with women
Or their shallow, giggling ways.
Then came the day
When I, retired and prosperous,
Was forced to ask myself: What now?
Where do I go from here?
And an instinct, generous and concerned,
Drove me to conclude I should return

And share my fortune with my family.
But first, some questions to be answered:
Did they still live, and – if so – in Knockore?
And – most importantly – had time and poverty
Brought *her* to such a frame of mind
As would make her truly grateful
For this unexpected windfall?
So I dispatched a man to Ireland,
A man discrete, incisive, probing,
Back to my native village.
He soon returned with the facts:
Yes – she still lived in Knockore,
Where many wondered that she yet retained
Much of her youthful beauty.
She had betrayed her vows, her church,
And every value
Handed down through generations;
She had remarried
To a man of modest means
And given *his* name to *my* two girls,
Who now had children of their own.
And when it was suggested to her
I might be living still
And anxious to return home,
Her response was such to show
That in all the intervening years
She hadn't changed at all:
'May he never see Knockore again,'
She said, 'nor anyone
That might bring tidings of him.'

How, now, am I to blame
If my old age is spent
Deepening into bitterness
At the thought of women's perfidy,
Their inconstancy,
Their consummate talent for betrayal?

Moss Hanley

The cynic Andy Boo says I'm the one
Who fathered little Mickeleen – Miss Cara's son.

He's wrong.

Wrong, too, is Charles McGettigan, when
He cites me as a charitable man.

Neither sinner nor saint am I,
But too cowardly and too shy
To face up to her and say:
'I'll love you till my dyin' day.'

SÉAMUS MAC AN TSIONNAIGH

Tipsy, for once, and somwhat maudlin,
In the Oh So Posh –
And amn't I entitled to be
On the night of my retirement
At the party thrown by my good friends,
My many friends,
Children who have become the parents
Of children who, too, have grown away
But have returned tonight to wish me well.
My head
Resting against the wall above the urinal
While I pee,
Barely clearing my shoes
(Ah! What a change is there!)
And I ask myself once again
Which is the more important,
Fact or myth,
If one is to explain
The wonder of these people
And how my soul responds to them?
Myth or fact?
Fionn with his motto
And his *abhainn dearg*,
Or Mickeen the Boaster pissing here beside me,
Famed for his claim that it was he
Who introduced the first zip-fastener to Knockore?
'A lovely party, Master,' he remarks,
'And I wish you many long and happy years –
Yourself and Eibhlís – in retirement.'

I scan his face:
Is it the face of Fionn Mac Cumhaill grown old?
A zip to fasten flies
Or a river red with blood?
'Mickeen,' I say, 'you have a face
That would embellish any myth.'
He smiles – and there's affection there.
'You'll be missed, Master,' he consoles.
'All the scholars you put through your hands
Say you'll be missed.'
'Thanks, Mickeen,' I reply. 'I'll miss the teaching, too.'
But it was surely time to go –
As surely as the Fianna must make way
For e-mail and the Internet,
While I fumble for my willy
And put him back. Soft.
As Eibhlís would say:
I had my day.

Hannah Grogan

Take my advice, Eibhlís,
And from day wan,
Insist that he keep his historian's nose
Out o' your kitchen,
Otherwise, now he's retired,
You'll have him snifflin' and snufflin' around you
Like a cranky toddler
That won't get out from under your legs,
While you're busy peelin' the spuds.
He'll drive' you to distraction
With all that yappin' about mit' 'n' fact.
There's nothin' worse than a man about the place,
Talkin' nonsense,
When there's a dinner to be got ready.
You were too accommodatin', Eibhlís,
As I've often told you,
Durin' the randy years when
All that was botherin' him was his nooky.
Now that he's gone in that department,
Don't make the same mistake
If he expects you to be interested
In a load o' codswallop
About a gang o' hooligans
In Ireland long ago.
Men are even extra-demandin'
When their energy shifts
To above from below.
'Tis then or ever they expect
To be pampered and mollycoddled

And listened to when they pontificate
About matters originatin' in the brain,
Of no interest to anyone except themselves.
Put the foot down from day wan, girl,
Or you'll never have a minute's peace again.

Séamus Mac An tSionnaigh

Which was the brightest star in all that firmament
Of brilliant scholars who later would become
Doctors and engineers, teachers and priests,
Writers and politicians? There were some
Whose fame would spread beyond our shores,
But there was one whose intellect
Was finer than all the rest. Though shy and withdrawn
And timid as a child, one could still detect
A special talent waiting to unfold.
Diffident as ever, he stands before me now,
Wishing me good luck on my retirement,
Remembering his schooldays, recalling how
Easy it was to get me telling stories –
His favourite was 'Setanta and the Hound'.
'I farm twenty-seven acres,' he informs me,
'All of it boggy land, and the ground
Is unable to absorb the constant Irish rain,
So there's poor reward for work. It's a Spartan life
In a remote, mountainous place,
And then there is the loneliness, though
I understand, given the circumstances, a wife
Is out of the question. Sometimes – on nights
I come home drunk – I turn to table or chair
And, in reproachful tones, pretend
I'm admonishing a son or daughter.
Or I take the brush and dance with it
And sing "My Love Is Like a Red, Red Rose",
But most often I envy Culainn –
Sheer, bloody begrudgery, I suppose.

But you have to hand it to him:
His hound is killed, he finds a son instead –
Some way to beat the loneliness!
As for Setanta, that precocious lad –
Look how he overcame, in later life,
As leader of the Red Branch Knights,
Not once but many times, those paralyzing fears
Of hounds that lurk in wait, and so fulfilled
The golden promise of his boyhood years.'

Kevin Hall

Whenever I hear mentioned
Saddam's most famous quote
About 'the Mother of all Wars',
I think of you
Standing over me, menacingly,
And ranting like an incoherent lunatic
As I go on my knees to weed
That field of turnips –
That one good acre of our twenty-seven.
'When I come back from the creamery,' you'd say
(Twelve hours late, drunk as a lord),
'I'm not to see as much as wan weed left.
If I do, you'll feel the back of my belt
Across your bare backside.
How is it I can't depend on you
To do that much right? It must be the books
Have made you into such a dulamoo.
Lord, what wouldn't I give for a young son
Who'd be said by me? And remember
To be careful as you weed:
There's not to be wan turnip plucked by mistake.
Can I trust you with that much, boy?
Or would you rather go to school
To hear the ravin's of oul' Mac An tSionnaigh,
Who wouldn't know a weed from a turnip
If the two of 'em was put in front of him?
A quare place this world would be
If all we had was masters and their scholars.
Who'd feed us then?

Who'd put the turnips on the table?
Drive thoughts of schooling from your head, my boy,
And stick instead to what you know,
And to what your father knows:
Wet fields and boggy land
And a patch of turnips ripe for weedin'.
That way, at least, you'll feed yourself.
And not one turnip by mistake, d'you hear?
Not one turnip by mistake, or you'll have
Nothin' to ate tomorrow. You'll learn from me
That wilful waste makes woeful want.'

Wilful waste makes woeful want.

Two things to note
About my father and Saddam:
They loved to terrorise,
And they were always good for a quote.

ANNA HALL

At two he had more words
Than most boys twice his age;
At three he knew all his prayers;
At five he was full of jokes;
At six he wrote me a poem
To thank me for a toy;

At twelve he was silent and unhappy.

That man has been forgiven much
But I'll see he suffers yet
For chasing the honeyed words
From my chatty boy.

GRACE HOPE (KILDARE)

Before he chased the honeyed words
And – for this be ever grateful –
For one last precious year
Before she died,
Mine was the name most mentioned
In your long conversations
When she'd reminisce, as she was wont to do,
About the happy times
Before she married
When we lodged together – two young working girls –
In Mount Pleasant Street in Dublin.

Grace and myself were at a dance
Where we met two gamey fellas . . .

And will I ever forget the night
Grace and myself got drunk for the first time . . .

Grace and myself would always paint the town
On pay-night . . .

And you listened in astonishment
That one now so defeated
Could once have been so happy.

And you conjured with my name:
Grace Hope.
Once upon a time there was
A ray of sunshine on a cloudy day,

A harbinger of grace and hope,
A spark of delight
Before the awful gloom.

And though you never met me,
You felt at times an overwhelming urge
To seek me out
And thank me.

You conjured with my name again today
When, going through her personal effects
In search of a photograph
For her mortuary card,
You came across one of herself and me.
At the back was written:
'Grace and myself – August '57'.

That photograph was taken
Just three days before
She first set eyes on him.
She'd fall in love,
Within six months they'd marry,
And she'd be gone
Out of my life forever.

Look at the photograph again:
Now, at last, we've come face to face.
Wasn't I pretty?
Yes, and full of devilment!
I'd just said something smutty
To the starchy old photographer,

And your mother, as you see, is bending
Over with convulsive laughter.

You wonder what became of me?
Suffice to say that I, too, fell in love,
And not all love stories
Have a sorry ending.

ARMAGH JOHN

You'd need a course in etiquette
Before coming to live here.

Can anyone say why
A customer should choose to be insulted
If I forget to shutter up my windows
Or lock my shopfront door
When her second cousin's funeral
Is passing by?

MICKEEN THE BOASTER

Can you stick out your tongue
In an upward loop
So that either side of it
Touches your upper lip?
You can?
Then rejoice that you're not numbered
Among the thirty per cent or so
Of God's creation
Who can't accomplish this simple feat.

Now:
Can you stick out your tongue
In a downward loop
So that either side of it
Touches the lower lip?
You can't?
Don't panic!
A hefty ninety-nine per cent
Are in the same predicament as you.

As for myself, of course,
I must not be counted
Among the generality of men . . .
I'm something special.

Watch my tongue! See!

Your common, lying braggart
Is expert at regaling

With claims that can't be verified.
I, for my part, will boast
Only of what is demonstrably true.

Watch my tongue again!

There is a special gene required
For this distinctive downward loop,
And only the chosen few are favoured.
Only a chosen few,
And I among them.

I've often asked myself
Why I should be so privileged.
I think, perhaps, the Lord has favoured us –
My forefathers and I –
Because, when we boast,
We never lie.

We use the tongue as God intended,
Letting our uniqueness do the talking.
Truly,
Why should we resort to falsehood
When, in our case,
The truth is more engaging?

All that I boast of may be verified.

Just one example:
The only Knockorian to be born
On the night of the Big Wind

Was my great-grandfather.
Such was the howling of the gale,
He had to bawl with all his might
To make his presence felt.
His lung-power, thus, developed in the cradle,
And this is why, in later life,
He could keep his head submerged
In a bucketful of water
For one hundred and twenty-seven seconds.

People came from far and near
To see 'the man with the fish's lung'.
Some who came would cast admiring glances
At the handsome young Knockorians;
Some would marry; some would settle here.
And, were I in the mind to boast tonight,
I could keep an audience entertained,
As I have often done, for hours on end,
With tales of how new blood was introduced,
Of how the history of Knockore was changed forever
By the lung-power of my ancestor.

Your genuine boast is always entertaining.

How blessed is Knockore to host
A family like mine,
So entertaining and so gifted
That others may delight in, marvel at
Our every boast.

JOE HAMMOND

The Tuesday game of Forty-one,
And, because 'tis pushin' up to Christmas,
Turkeys instead of chickens for the winners.

The game most delicately poised:
First to reach three takes home the bird.
We're two games all, and now, in the decider,
Myself is twenty-six and lookin' good;
Mickeen the Boaster stands at twenty bare,
With Bosco Collins bringin' up the rear
At sweet sixteen.

My deal. I turn the Ace of Clubs and rob.
My hand is very promisin'
For, with the Ace, I have the King and Queen,
With the Deuce and Three as backers.

Bosco leads with the Ten o' Spades,
Mickeen shoots in the Four o' Clubs to me;
I hit it with the three. I'm thirty-wan.

I lead the Ace; Bosco's Seven falls.
Mickeen reneges; I'm thirty six
And into the home stretch.

It's lookin' good; it's lookin' good enough
To make a man feel, well, superior.
I can't resist the urge
To drive that feelin' home.

'Mickeen,' I say, "tis commonly reported
That your great-grandfather with the fish's lung
Wasn't half the man that he's cracked up to be.'
From the way he straightens himself,
'Tis easy t'see
That knocks a hop out o' him.

"Tis said he hadn't near the pullin' power
You claim he had, and that he only brought
Wan family – the Hansons – to Knockore.'

By now there's temper in his eyes. Good.

I lead the King.
Bosco can only drop the Six. He's gone.
'And what about the Tom Pateens?'
Says Mickeen, knucklin' my King hard
With the Five o' Trumps;

'And what about the Butty Gilfoyles?'
He pounds the Jack on the table,
Makin' the cards hop,
And sweeps my Two;

'And what about the squint-eyed Coyles?'
He bangs the table with the Ace o' Hearts
So hard the glasses dance,
And sweeps my last remainin' Queen.

He's forty-wan: the bird is his.

'Enjoy your pandy for tomorrow's dinner,'
He advises me, as he bags his prize.
'It might stop you talkin' through your arse.'

EILEEN GILFOYLE

You can, if you're an innocent,
Believe Mickeen the Boaster speaks the truth.

You can accept
That when the three Moran sisters –
Siobhan, Josephine and Anne –
Dressed up in their finest
And started out on the five-mile walk
From the Gale to Knockore,
On August fifteenth, 1951,
All they had in mind was to gawk
At the man with the fish's lung.

You can, if you're so inclined,
Marvel at the lucky chance
That brought the three strong farmers
From the surrounding hinterland
Into Knockore village that same day.

And you might find appealing
The story of the blossoming of love
Among the three Gale sisters and these men –
Love of such intensity
No dowry was required,
Unless one takes the absolute condition
That sons born of each wedlock
Would forsake forever more
The black and red of the Gale
For the blue and white of Knockore.

Or you can take one look at me,
At my tall, stately figure,
My milk-white complexion,
My sloe-black hair,
At the beauty bequeathed by
Siobhan Moran, my grandmother.

Then you can read the Book of Genesis
And believe a different kind of truth:
Three women, graceful and alluring,
Offering, apparently in all innocence,
Their version of forbidden fruit
To three men dancing to an impulse
Insistent, savage and enduring.

SIOBHAN GILFOYLE (NÉE MORAN)

Does anyone, I wonder, understand
The poverty of way-back-then?
Or that, because we came
From the hungry side of a mountain,
We didn't have a choice when our three men
Came riding into town?
The one who fell for me
Was on the short side.
I remember the first time we kissed
I had to bow my head, and even then
He had to stand on tippy-toes.
Had the choice been mine,
He'd not have figured on my list.

And look at all that I'd have missed.

JOSEPHINE COYLE (NÉE MORAN)

He was the plainest of the three,
And bald and squinty-eyed;
But then again, ninety-two
Acres of the very best of land
Had a way of helping me decide
He'd do.

ANNE HALE (NÉE MORAN)

For the whole of our courtship
There was hardly a word out of him,
He was so shy and, I think,
So overawed by my beauty.
But then – our wedding night in bed!
Have you ever seen a weasel
After a rat? Nothing in this world
Will come between him and his prey.
My shy killer made each day
A waiting for the night ahead.

BUTTY GILFOYLE

There I was, having my quiet pint
In the Oh So Posh
When this well-dressed and pretty young wan,
Smellin' of powder and perfume,
Accosted me.
'Mr Gilfoyle,' she said, 'I've just been told the story
Of how, fifty years ago, you met your wife,
Though, in the circumstances,
"Met" is hardly the word that I should choose –
And, please take note, women today
Do have won the right to choose.
"Bought" would seem more appropriate,
For that is what you did, sir:
You bought her just as certainly
As any common huckster
Might purchase cattle at a fair.
I'm told she was a beauty in her day
And towered above you
Not just physically, but in every way
That intelligence and grace
Lords it over the commonplace.
One can only guess
As to the loss of dignity
And the deep unhappiness
Endured by countless women
Such as your good wife,
Forced by the ravages of poverty
To stoop into a loveless married life.'

Later, when I got home,
Herself was watching something on TV,
So I upped and told her
Of this latest incident.
She was, at first, more interested
In the bloody box than me.
'Will you listen, woman, to what I have to say
About the young wan that accosted me this day?'
I had to plead. And so, at last, she did;
She heard me out with great attention
To every detail and then asked,
'Did this young wan happen to mention
Her name, by any chance?
Or where she came from,
Or her business here?'
'If she did, I didn't bring it with me,'
I replied. 'And anyway,
What has that got to do with it?'
'It has everything to do with it,' she said.
'She must be a stranger in the place,
To say that you don't know her.
A stranger in Knockore?
And all dressed up in finery?
And smellin' nice with perfume?
And pretty, too, to boot? Now, where
Did you come across the likes of that before?
You can be sure
She's not here for the scenery.
Romance is in the air.
But aren't you the world's worst,' she said,
'For bringin' only half the story,

And we don't come across the better half
Until 'tis far too late
And all the kick is gone from it.
Th' other day you came home with the news
That Tansy Holly had her baby girl,
But did you bring the infant's name and weight?'

BUTTY GILFOYLE

Siobhan! Put on the glasses, quick!
Here, in today's *Kerryman*,
There's a snap of the pretty young wan
That launched a broadside at me yesterday.
Her name is Amanda Concita Lovelace,
And there she is, standin', proud as punch,
Beside young David Harrington,
Our new solicitor, who's holdin'
A little wan dressed only in a nappy.
'David and Amanda,' it says here,
'Are to be married next week
In Paddington, London,
He for the first time, she for the third,
And they're both
Deliriously happy.'

SIOBHAN GILFOYLE

What did I tell you, Butty?
What did I say
About the bit o' romance?
They're all talkin' about the great changes
That are takin' place.
But some things never change, love;
They're still the same old way
As they were in our time,
And men are still compelled to answer
Women who give the come-hither.

LUKE COYLE

I can't sing.
Or make up songs of love.
My words are plain as my bald head
And my notes, like my squinty eyes,
Are inclined to drift
In and out of focus.

So, you ask me if I know
'Twas land that first decided her:
Of course I do.
'Twas hardly my good looks
Or my poetic style
That brought her here that day
All of fifty years ago.
But here's my question, now:
What persuaded her to stay?

Not havin' the words,
Not havin' the notes,
I won't attempt to answer that one.

Just let me say,
Over the passing years,
I got to know her well –
As well as she knows me.
The knowing pleased the both of us.
Is that love?
There's a question, now,
More suited to philosophy

Than to an ignorant,
Unlettered farmer the likes of me,
Who works the land each day,
Waitin' for the dusk, when I will bring
Home to her talk of sick cows
Or promisin' young heifers.

What else can I do
When I can't sing?

TOM PATEEN HALE

The psychologist on TV
Used big words and lovely phrases
When arguing against the whole idea
Of marriage bureaus.
He spoke about 'the sad manipulation
Of people in need'
And 'the dark and mercenary convergence
Of lust and poverty'.

The man set me thinkin'.

Was it lust that sent me scamperin' to you?
You can be sure it was.
And poverty that first brought you this way?
The answer must be 'Yes'.

But what was sad about it?

Weren't you always contented here,
Away from the daily grind
Of scrapin' out a hungry livin',
Mistress of your patch,
And free to come and go?

How often have you told me so?

And how often have we laughed
As I described
(Mostly, as I tickled you in bed)

The lusty fires that started
Burnin' in my loins
And the sinful thoughts
That went coursin' through my head
The first time I saw you?
Lust is too weak a word for it!
I said to myself
That August day in 1951:
'She's beautiful!
She's absolutely beautiful!
And the whole bloody farm,
The house and all,
Can go up in scutterin' smoke
For all I care,
So long as I can bed
That noble woman there.'

Of course, being the cagey type,
And in mortal dread
That you'd bolt if you got wan hint
Of the lustiness of my intent,
I kept all these randy thoughts
Within the confines of my own head.
You only saw the shy boy,
Full of manners and politeness,
Mumbling his words of introduction:
'Er, p-p-p-pleased to meet you, miss,'
Is all I think I said.

ANNE PATEEN HALE

Indeed, the only thing that's sad about it
Is that, after all the years,
Your lust has waned,
Though, never one for useless tears,
You choose instead to joke about it.

It takes me all night now
To do just wance
What wance I did all night.

I'll never be as good
As wance I was,
But I'm as good wance
As ever I was.

My love!
They were great nights!
Part of the – if you'll excuse the pun –
Delightful bonding process
Between man and wife.

And isn't it nice to think
That even now, every once in a blue moon,
You and your 'dotey little trollop'
Can still raise a bit of a gallop?

TOMMY TAYLOR

They started up a boxing club,
And just because I'm extra tall
And thick around the shoulders,
They said I could box heavyweight.

They put me in the ring
With this fearsome-looking monster,
And when the first bell sounded,
He cracked me such a thump
That my stomach scraped my spine.
I crumpled on the floor
But was up at the count of eight.
'Box on, box on,' waved the referee.

'You can box him yourself,' says I,
Vaultin' over the highest rope,
Clear out of the ring.

No sooner had I bolted from the hall
Than they christened me
'The Great White Hope'.

ENDA SPILLANE

Twenty years ago today, St Patrick's Day,
As we had a kick-around in the football field,
A row between the pair of us
Got out of hand,
And we fought it out, tooth and nail.

I was the best scrapper in the boxing club,
But temper made a different man of him,
And with one vicious punch
He flattened me. Dazed
As I was, I still remember
The face contorted, the eyes crazed
With bloodlust. Others held him back
As he moved in for the kill.

Yesterday, I gave him a lift from Dublin
And – yes, it's true – the nerves
Are playing Molly Bawn with him.

Somewhere outside Nenagh
A sparrow came from nowhere,
Tossed itself against my windscreen
With a light thump
And was gone.

For the next three miles he begged and pleaded
That I return to the scene,
And when, weary at last, I consented,
He sought out and found the little creature,
And cupped it gently in his hand.

'I'm glad our feathered friend is dead.
Now we can rest at ease;
Now we know
It didn't have to suffer,' he said.

Moss Hanley

The first customer in
After I'd put up my 'Closing Down Sale' sign
Was Mike Hally – a man I hadn't seen
For the best part of twelve months.
He said 'twas a sin
To see so many have to shut their door,
And if this continued
There'd be nothin' left of Knockore.
'If the small shops go,
The village won't be far behind'
Was his theme as he fished around,
Takin' his time, on a sharp lookout
For the very best bargains.
'Would you believe,' he said,
That you are the twelfth in seven years
To put the shutters up? There's only five
Left now where wance you had twenty-five.
Where's it all going to end, I ask myself,
Or will there be no shopkeepers soon
To keep an open stall?'
As he stuffed his goodies,
Every one of them a give-away,
Into his huge shopping bag, marked
'Dunnes Stores Better Value Beats Them All'.

MOSS HANLEY

He turned on his way out,
Held up his bag of goodies, and said:
'Seein' as 'tis comin' up to Santy
And you'll be closed for the New Year,
Is there any chance of a free
Christmas box with these
To celebrate the season of good cheer?'

Cara Evans

'Tis fine for Mike Gavin and his likes:
They have the motor cars
To take 'em to Tralee,
Where they can get their bargains.
But what about the likes of me,
That's grounded in Knockore?
Will somebody tell me how
I'm supposed to travel for my shoppin'
Or where on earth
I'll get the bit of credit now?

Jack the Ram

They're all the time complainin'
About the drop in population
And the school numbers fallin'
And the small shops closin'.

I have the answer
For two out of the three:

Tell 'em to ferry
The women on to me.

MIKE HALLY

My question is: why can't
Those who say that I'm a miser
Understand that hunger in a ten-year-old
Affects the brain forever,
Or that nightmares can be driven
By the fear of want?

JIM THE RUBBISH MAN

Whatever you do, Mac An tSionnaigh,
When you write the latest history of this place
And the story of our closing shops
And our empty classrooms, our deserted streets,
And our fall from grace
Among the literati who see us now
As superstitious backwoodsmen
Out of step with the times,
Espousing an antiquated religion
In post-Catholic Ireland –
Whatever you do then,
Don't, for the love of God,
Go sentimental.
None of your bullshit, please,
About our likes not being seen again.
Where's your Knockorian sense of humour, man!
So – concede their every argument
About this economic backwater;
Tell 'em that we apologise
For our location on the map,
That we go to our graves
Sorry we're not from Dublin
And that we deeply regret any offence
We caused the sneering journalist
Who foraged here to gather
What might fill a page with mockery.
Don't dare to mention
The bright young men and women
Who, each weekend, return

In jam-packed busloads,
Rejecting the enlightened
And politically correct metropolis
For a dose of devilment,
Nor say, wherever men conspire
Around a winter fire
To tell fantastic tales
Of errant wives
Or husbands cuckolded,
Knockore still lives.

Josie McBride

Out of the blue this morning,
I began to think of Suzy Honan,
My childhood pal, who, suddenly, in '47,
Left, and vanished forever without trace.
Where is she now, I wondered,
And why did she never write?
And does she even know her parents died?
And if she knew, why didn't she come home
To see them laid to rest?

And there was one abiding memory.

It was a summer Sunday,
Just weeks before her unexpected leaving.
We were two sixteen-year-olds
Walking on the river bank
On a path no longer used,
So that we had to beat our way
Through briar and bramble.
Our legs were torn and scratched
But we persisted,
Driven, as sometimes youngsters are,
By the fear of turning back.
'Wouldn't it be great,' said Suzy,
'If we discovered something strange or frightening
In this forgotten place –
A secret hideaway for lovers,
And maybe a knife there, stained with faded blood,
Or even the remains of human bones,

So that we'd be wondering
If a lovers' quarrel
Ended in a bloody tragedy.'

We journeyed on, excited and afraid;
We walked until we were exhausted,
But we found nothing, nothing at all,
Except the thorny briar and bramble.

'We'd better turn back,' she said at last,
Disappointment written on her face.
There was silence on the way home,
Which she broke only once to complain:
'Nothing dangerous or exciting ever happens
In this godforsaken place.'

MAUDY FERGUSON (NEW YORK)

This city never sleeps;
Just as the Shannon tumbles on the shore,
And then retreats,
And then returns
And spills itself again
At Bunaclogga Bay,
So the millions of New York
Keep coming and going
Always and forever,
Night and day,
Intent and bustling as the Shannon river.

Through the window of my apartment
Comes the constant hooting of the trains.
It has been a hard day,
But how, amid the din, can I find rest?
Let me pretend, let me pretend
I'm listening to the sound that I love best:
The Shannon washing on the shore
At Bunaclogga, where the curlews keep
A lonely vigil, their plaintive cries
Reaching, on a calm night,
The village of Knockore.

I fall asleep.

LINDA FOWLER

Who should walk into my office this very morning
But Maudy Ferguson,
Looking somewhat dejected, I thought,
Though she soon perked up
When we chatted and bantered
About the folks back home
And all the fun we'd had
In our childhood village of Knockore.

'We must meet again,' I suggested,
'For a meal and a night on the town.
We must talk some more.'

Then, as she was about to leave, she said,
'I hear you've done very well for yourself.'
'Not too badly,' I replied.
'I'm personnel manager here:
 My job is to hire and fire.'

'Could I have a job?' she asked.

'Unfortunately, Maudy,' I lied,
'There's nothing available just now,
Though, of course, I'll keep you in mind.'

How was I to tell her
That I'm paid to be unpopular,
That I must drive the workers
Until every limb is sore?

Being the bitch doesn't bother me at all,
Though I draw the line
With people from Knockore.

ORLA SHINE (STORE SALESPERSON)

I'd highly recommend that suite of furniture
You're eying there, ma'am.
It's as good as new,
Hardly ever used, and going as second-hand.
The lady who returned it
Told me she'd spent most of her life
Scrimping and scraping,
With only one thing in mind –
To come back home.
Built a beautiful house in the old place,
Nothing only the best by way of furnishings,
But somehow couldn't settle.
She was thinking, maybe
It was the quietness that got to her
After all the noise of Boston,
And she was dismayed to find
She was always talking to strangers,
Children and grandchildren
Of childhood friends
Who were all gone.
Even the place itself had changed, she said.
Many of the houses she had known were down
And – would you believe,
This is what hurt her most of all –
There used to be a stream
Where, half a century ago, she fished for minnows –
It's filthy and dead now.

I'll be leaving for Boston tomorrow,' she told me.
'I should never have returned.
That way, at least,
I'd still be able to dream.'

JOEY HOURIGAN

Since Andy touched the seventy,
He's crankier than ever.
Just last night he drank till he was senseless,
And then proceeded to insult us all:
'Bloody hypocrites, the lot of ye,' he said,
'Beatin' the breast in the church on Sunday,
And livin' like pagans for the six days followin'.
Three score and ten I've lived here,
Never been beyond Tralee,
And all I say is, not wance in all that time
Did I see in this benighted village
Wan daycent Christian act of charity.'
On he went like that,
Repeatin' himself over and over.
The insults we could take in our stride,
But he kept buttin' in with the same oul' complaint,
Makin' it impossible for us to chat,
Which tested our patience to the limit.
Then, to crown it all, as he was going
To the jacks, he staggered and fell
And, before anyone could catch him,
He cracked his poll wickedly off the floor.

We had to lift him home
And wash away the blood,
And bandage his cut head,
And take off his clothes
And put him to bed.

KNOCKORE CHURCH

Suppose Andy Boo is right,
Suppose those who come here to pray
Are the blackest transgressors of all,
Whose sins, in the light of day,

Would draw blushes from Satan himself;
Suppose that among those who come
Is the gossip with words that can kill
With a rattlesnake flick of the tongue;

And the vulgar man, common and loud;
And the randy man, bent on his thrill;
And the sly one whose sins are unknown,
Being hidden with devious skill;

And the openly scandalous man
Ever ready to boast of his fall;
Suppose only these come to pray;
Still, I welcome them all.

And I welcome the vain man, too,
Who assumes a posture of prayer;
And the proud one who struts down my aisle
With a haughty, superior air;

And I welcome the judgemental one
Who pronounces what others should do;
And when the imposter shows up,
I welcome him too.

Yes, I welcome the children of Eve,
Sad victims of sin and the Fall,
For, were I to wait for the saint,
I'd have no one to welcome at all.